Whisky

Sous la direction de Thierry Benitah & Bastien Demnard, La Maison du Whisky
Rédaction : Éric Chenebier, Jean-Marc Bellier, Thierry Benitah & Bastien Demnard
Relecture technique : Bastien Demnard
Conception graphique et mise en pages : Delphine Delastre pour Flammarion
Responsable éditoriale : Ryma Bouzid-Fuchs
Fabrication : Christelle Lemonnier
Photogravure : IGS, L'Isle d'Espagnac

N° d'édition française : L.01EPMN000945.N001
ISBN : 978-2-0814-1634-5

Distributed in English as *Whisky: The Connoisseur's Journal*
Editorial Director: Kate Mascaro
Editor: Helen Adedotun
Translated from the French by David Radzinowicz
Copyediting: Anne McDowall
Proofreading: Samuel Wythe
Jacket illustrations © Nimaxs / Shutterstock.com

English edition #: L.01EBTN000807.N001
ISBN: 978-2-08-020339-7

Flammarion, S.A.
87, quai Panhard et Levassor
75647 Paris Cedex 13
France
editions.flammarion.com

Dépôt légal : 10/2017

17 18 19 3 2 1

La Maison du Whisky

WHISKY

Flammarion

How To Enjoy Whisky

Du plaisir du whisky

INTRODUCTION

Recently, sorting through a closet in the family home, I stumbled across my very first wine journal. It was just a folder with pages containing dozens of labels accompanied by annotations and a few tasting notes. One of these labels had been carefully peeled off a bottle of Saint-Émilion 1970, enjoyed one Sunday in August 1980, whose aroma of violets had sent me into raptures. Better still, at the back, I found receipts of my earliest purchases, with which I had quickly built up a rather eclectic cellar.

In a second notebook, I came across anecdotes recalling times I had spent with extraordinary wine producers who I had met in vineyards all over France. It brought back memories of my meetings with personalities such as Jacques Reynaud of Château Rayas in Châteauneuf du Pape; Pierre Overnoy of Arbois-Pupillin—one of the pioneers of biodynamics in France; Alain Vauthier of Château Ausone; as well as Corinne Dupuy of the Domaine Labranche-Laffont, in the Madiran appellation; and others who had seen fit to share with me a little of their expertise and their passion.

Their passion was not limited to wine, however. The first question Jacques Reynaud asked me was, "Do you know Michel Couvreur's whiskies?" Which is how I discovered the legendary Belgian independent bottler based in Burgundy who has done so much to encourage the appreciation of whisky in France. It was also a single malt that got me into the merry band of disinterested enthusiasts who write for the wine periodical *Le Rouge et le Blanc*. I had advised one of its members to try the extraordinary Ledaig 1972 bottled by La Maison du Whisky; in return he invited me to join the independent review, which is today,

PRÉAMBULE

Tout dernièrement, en rangeant l'une des armoires de la maison familiale, je suis tombé sur mon premier livre de cave. Il s'agissait d'un simple classeur, dont les pages rassemblaient des dizaines d'étiquettes accompagnées d'annotations et de quelques notes de dégustation. L'une d'entre elles avait été soigneusement décollée d'une bouteille de Saint-Émilion 1970, bue un dimanche d'août 1980, et dont le parfum de violette m'avait enthousiasmé. Mieux encore, je retrouvais en annexe les factures des premiers achats qui m'avaient permis de me constituer rapidement une cave plutôt éclectique.

Dans un second cahier, je retrouvais des anecdotes évoquant les moments partagés avec des vignerons extraordinaires, rencontrés dans différents vignobles français. J'y revivais mes plus belles rencontres avec des personnalités telles que Jacques Reynaud, du Château Rayas, sur Châteauneuf du Pape, Pierre Overnoy, d'Arbois-Pupillin, l'un des pionniers de la biodynamie en France, Alain Vauthier, du Château Ausone, ou encore Corinne Dupuy, du Domaine Labranche-Laffont, sur l'appellation Madiran et bien d'autres qui avaient accepté de partager avec moi un peu de leur expertise et de leur passion.

Une passion qui ne se limitait pas au vin. En effet, la première question que me posa Jacques Reynaud fut : « Connaissez-vous les whiskies de Michel Couvreur ? ». C'est ainsi que je découvris le légendaire embouteilleur indépendant belge, basé en Bourgogne, qui a tant fait pour l'appréciation du whisky en France. Ce fut également un single malt qui me permit de rejoindre la bande de passionnés désintéressés de *Le Rouge et le Blanc* : j'avais conseillé à l'un de ses membres l'extraordinaire Ledaig 1972, embou-

more than ever, committed to combating uniformity and lack of character in wine.

It was later, toward the end of the 1980s, while managing a Parisian cellar, that I was able to really learn about whisky. The experience made such an impact on me that it changed the course of my career forever. In one day, my eyes sparkling and my taste buds tingling with wonder, I discovered miracles such as Lagavulin 12 Year Old (with its brown label), Talisker 8 Year Old, Springbank 21 Year Old, Caol Ila 12 Year Old, The Macallan 18 Year Old, Highland Park 12 Year Old, and Laphroaig 10 Year Old, as well as the very first cask-strength bottlings or those labeled "Prestonfield" by Scottish independent bottler Signatory Vintage, along with many other incredible single malts. Following these revelations, I started reading up on the subject and tasting in earnest, meeting countless connoisseurs, and gradually ascending from the status of neophyte to that of expert.

One of my most priceless memories dates to 2005. Thierry Bénitah, chairman of La Maison du Whisky, and I were selecting a single malt, unaware that a few months later it would be voted best whisky of the year. It was the Laphroaig 1974, a blend of two sherry casks released in a limited series of 910 bottles. We had begun by tasting a sample from a first cask: it was superb, teeming with flavors of peat, camphor, iodine, and salt, but lacking the enduring trademark of a great Laphroaig—an exotic fruitiness (mango, passion fruit) overflowing with vitality, combined with an irresistible chocolaty mellowness. These very qualities were all present in the second cask, but that single malt lacked power. At our request, the two casks were blended. The osmosis was perfection itself: the miracle had worked.

Wine and whisky: I have been immensely fortunate to be able to enjoy my dual passions simultaneously.

teillé par La Maison du Whisky, à la suite de quoi il m'avait invité à rejoindre la revue indépendante, qui contribue aujourd'hui plus que jamais à lutter contre la banalisation des vins.

Plus tard, vers la fin des années 1980, c'est en devenant responsable d'une cave parisienne que j'ai pu véritablement m'initier à l'univers du whisky. Le choc fut tel qu'il bouleversa mon parcours professionnel. Au cours d'une même journée, je découvris, regard et palais émerveillés, Lagavulin 12 ans (étiquette marron), Talisker 8 ans, Springbank 21 ans, Caol Ila 12 ans, The Macallan 18 ans, Highland Park 12 ans, Laphroaig 10 ans, ainsi que les tous premiers embouteillages brut de fûts ou estampillés « Prestonfield » du négociant écossais Signatory Vintage et tant d'autres single malts... Après cette révélation, je me plongeais corps et âme dans les lectures et les dégustations et multipliais les rencontres, passant ainsi du statut de novice à celui d'expert !

L'un de mes plus beaux souvenirs date de 2005. Thierry Bénitah, le PDG de La Maison du Whisky, et moi-même avions alors sélectionné un single malt sans savoir qu'il allait devenir, quelques mois plus tard, le meilleur whisky de l'année ! Il s'agissait du Laphroaig 1974, série limitée à 910 bouteilles, issue de l'assemblage de deux fûts ayant contenu du sherry. Nous avions tout d'abord dégusté l'échantillon d'un premier fût superbe, aux arômes de tourbe, de camphre, d'iode et de sel, mais auquel il manquait la marque de fabrique des grands Laphroaig : un exotisme fruité (mangue, passion) débordant de vitalité associé à une suavité chocolatée irrésistible. Or ces qualités étaient toutes présentes dans un second fût dont le single malt manquait, lui, de puissance. À notre demande, on assembla les deux fûts. L'osmose se révéla parfaite, le miracle avait eu lieu...

Vin et whisky, j'avais l'immense bonheur de vivre

However, although it seemed obvious to me back then that I should keep an up-to-date connoisseur's journal for my Burgundies, Bordeaux, and wines from the Jura, the idea of indulging in the same practice for whisky did not even enter my head: my precious tasting notes were enough for me.

WHY KEEP A WHISKY JOURNAL?

Today, the creation of a journal dedicated to whisky seems indispensable for two basic reasons. First and foremost, it allows one to combine a passion for whisky with the act of writing: by taking the time to note down a few words on a page, you prolong the pleasure of each tasting. It is also a way to relive all of those marvelous memories squirreled away over the years in the deepest recesses of the mind, for which whisky acts as a bridge between the past, the present, and even the future.

Over the last thirty years, the world of whisky has undergone a metamorphosis. In the past, whisky lovers would purchase a single malt or a blend simply to drink it. Nowadays, the pleasure of acquiring an exceptional bottle and tasting it together with other knowledgeable souls has become widespread among a number of enthusiasts, and there are now numerous collectors of premium bottles.

This connoisseur's journal is intended to act as a guide and mentor for your olfactory and gustatory memory. It will also serve to record a vast range of emotions: a hint of nostalgia, certainly, but also much pleasure, happiness, and astonishment, as well as moments of pride and even those touches of spirituality without which the world of whisky would not exert the same attraction.

pleinement deux passions en même temps. Pourtant, à l'époque, s'il me paraissait évident de tenir à jour un livre de cave pour recenser mes bourgognes, mes bordeaux, mes vins du Jura... l'idée d'en faire autant pour le whisky ne m'avait pas effleuré l'esprit : mon précieux carnet de dégustation me suffisait.

POURQUOI UN LIVRE DE CAVE ?

Aujourd'hui, la création d'un livre de cave dédié au whisky me paraît indispensable pour deux raisons essentielles. C'est d'abord l'occasion d'associer cette passion au geste d'écriture, de prendre le temps de tracer des mots sur une page et de prolonger ainsi le plaisir procuré par chaque dégustation. C'est également un moyen de revivre de merveilleux moments emmagasinés, au fil des années, au plus profond de notre mémoire, le whisky faisant le lien entre le passé, le présent et même l'avenir.

L'univers du whisky a considérablement évolué au cours des trente dernières années. Jadis, les amateurs achetaient leurs single malts et autres blends avant tout pour les boire. Aujourd'hui, le plaisir d'acquérir une bouteille d'exception et de la déguster en compagnie d'autres amateurs est désormais partagé par un nombre croissant de passionnés et on ne compte plus le nombre de collectionneurs qui accumulent ces bouteilles.

Ce livre de cave servira de fil d'Ariane à votre mémoire olfactive et gustative. Il sera également appelé à recueillir une vaste gamme d'émotions : un peu de nostalgie, certes, mais aussi beaucoup de plaisir, de bonheur et de surprise, sans oublier des moments de fierté et même une certaine forme de spiritualité sans laquelle le monde du whisky n'exercerait pas un tel attrait.

HOW TO USE THIS CONNOISSEUR'S JOURNAL

Whether you record your bottles progressively, by date of purchase, or according to some other, more complex method of classification, keeping a journal does call for a modicum of rigor.

While tasting, it is imperative to write down every impression, every perception—even the most fleeting—immediately. To add a little spice and flavor to your notes, I also recommend that you make a record of the circumstances under which and with whom you enjoyed the whisky.

Each page in the "Cellar Notes" section (pp. 61-168) is divided into two parts. The first comprises a detailed identification sheet that will enable you to draw up an identikit picture of each bottle tasted. This is the objective part of a journal or cellar book, its backbone. It is important to note down all available information as conscientiously as possible, since in time even the tiniest detail may become relevant.

The second part of the page is for critical notes; this is the place where you can allow free rein to the expression of your palate and your personality. It represents the subjective and emotional part of what is your journal. In certain cases, a single word may say more than an entire paragraph, while on other occasions a whole page won't be enough to quench your thirst for writing. The only rule worth following is to dispense with all rules. Gauging your expertise is not the point: just write down freely and sincerely whatever the whisky in question inspires.

COMMENT UTILISER CE LIVRE DE CAVE ?

Que vous répertoriez vos bouteilles au fur et à mesure, par date d'achat, ou selon une méthode de classement plus complexe, la tenue d'un livre de cave nécessite un minimum de rigueur. Ainsi, il est important de noter sans délai chaque impression, chaque perception ressentie (même la plus fugace) lors d'une dégustation. Pour ajouter encore plus de saveur et de piquant à vos notes, je vous recommande également de préciser dans quelles circonstances et avec qui le whisky a été partagé.

Dans la rubrique « Notes de cave » (pp. 61-168), chaque page comprend deux parties. La première est une fiche signalétique détaillée qui vous permettra de dresser un portrait-robot de chaque bouteille dégustée. C'est la part objective de tout livre de cave, sa colonne vertébrale. Il est donc important de noter ces informations aussi consciencieusement que possible, chaque détail pouvant se révéler de la plus grande pertinence au fil du temps.

Dédiée aux commentaires critiques, la seconde partie de la page permettra à chacun de laisser libre cours à l'expression de sa personnalité et de son palais. Elle représente la part subjective et émotionnelle de *votre* livre de cave. Dans certains cas, un mot en dit plus long qu'un chapitre complet, tandis qu'à d'autres occasions, une page entière ne suffira pas à étancher votre soif d'écrire. La seule règle à suivre est de ne pas avoir de règle. Peu importe l'expertise, écrivez librement et sincèrement en fonction de ce que le whisky vous inspire.

HOW TO STORE WHISKY

A whisky cellar generally contains three categories of bottles:

• **The cellar staples:** Everyday whiskies; bottles bought on the spur of the moment that can be drunk without much ceremony

• **Fine bottles:** Relatively rare, these are whiskies to keep for special occasions

• **Exceptional whiskies:** These collector's items are so precious that they should be tasted only very occasionally and only with genuine connoisseurs

Whatever the category, though, your whisky will require certain precautions to keep it in optimal condition.

Above all, it is important to know that **whisky bottles must imperatively be stored upright and never on their side,** because the cork will not hold-up for long against the attack of a spirit that boasts at least 40% alcohol (and which can sometimes exceed 60%).

This basic principle aside, however, it should be stressed that bottles of whisky, unlike wine, don't need to be stored in a cool, dark, and damp cellar. Many whisky lovers have a piece of furniture similar to a bookcase custom built and installed in their home to store and display their bottles.

However, a number of rules do need to be respected, similar to those that apply to wine, namely:

• **Ensure a stable temperature |** Avoid significant and sudden variations in temperature at all costs. Fluctuations between 50°F and 70°F (12°C and 20°C) are entirely acceptable. For a cellar in an apartment, a temperature below 70°F (20°C) is ideal.

COMMENT CONSERVER SES WHISKIES ?

Une cave à whisky comprend généralement trois catégories de bouteilles:

• **Un fond de cave :** il réunit les whiskies du quotidien, les bouteilles que l'on achète sans s'y arrêter et que l'on prend plaisir à déguster sans cérémonial.

• **Les belles bouteilles :** parfois plus rares, ce sont celles que l'on réserve à des moments ou à des événements précis.

• **Les whiskies d'exception :** ces pièces de collection sont d'une valeur telle qu'elles ne seront dégustée que très rarement, entre connaisseurs avertis.

Quelle que soit leur catégorie, vos whiskies demandent certaines précautions pour être conservées dans les meilleures conditions.

Avant tout, il est bon de rappeler que **toute bouteille de whisky doit impérativement être entreposée debout** et jamais couchée, car le bouchon ne résisterait pas longtemps aux assauts d'un breuvage qui titre au minimum 40 % (et peut parfois dépasser allègrement les 60 %).

Ce principe de base énoncé, il faut également souligner qu'à la différence du vin, il n'est pas nécessaire de posséder une cave fraîche, sombre et humide pour entreposer ses bouteilles de whisky. Beaucoup d'amateurs se font en effet construire des meubles sur mesure, parfois de véritables bibliothèques, dans une pièce de leur appartement ou de leur maison, pour y conserver leurs bouteilles et les mettre en valeur.

Toutefois, certaines règles à respecter sont proches de celles qui s'appliquent aux vins, à savoir :

• **Assurez une température stable.** L'essentiel est d'éviter à tout prix des variations importantes et subites de température. Des variations progressives

• **Choose a well-aired location with around 70% humidity** | Confined places are to be avoided at all cost as they can affect the cork and thereby mar the taste of the whisky. Ventilation to allow the air to circulate is recommended. In terms of humidity, be aware that a cellar that is too dry is bad for the stoppers and can cause the liquid inside the bottle to evaporate. On the other hand, excessive moisture can quickly damage the labels. To avoid this, you can buy transparent electrostatic film that protects both stopper and label.

• **Shade is best** | As with wine, whisky bottles are best stored in a dark place. Install low-intensity light bulbs and avoid neon lighting. Direct sunlight is particularly harmful. A simple and effective way to protect your whisky is to keep it in its original—and often attractive—case or box. This will also enhance the value of collectors' bottles, particularly at auction houses and on online auction websites.

The widely held opinion is that, once bottled, spirits such as whisky cease aging. This is not entirely false, but many specialists are convinced that over time air does succeed in seeping into the bottle through the stopper. They argue that this permits a beneficial process of micro-oxygenation to take place that continues to alter and refine the range of flavors and aromas of the whisky, as well as enhancing the mouthfeel.

One final word of advice: if you decide to custom-build storage furniture, make sure it is fitted with shelving that is both wide enough and adjustable, because whisky bottles come in many different shapes and sizes.

entre 12 °C et 20 °C sont tout à fait acceptables. Dans le cas d'une cave d'appartement, une température ne dépassant pas 20 °C est idéale.

• **Choisissez un lieu aéré, avec un taux d'humidité voisin de 70 %.** Évitez absolument les endroits confinés susceptibles de parasiter le goût du whisky à travers le bouchon. Pour cela, une bonne ventilation permet de brasser l'air ambiant. Pour ce qui est de l'hygrométrie, sachez qu'une cave trop sèche est préjudiciable aux bouchons et peut provoquer une évaporation du liquide à l'intérieur de la bouteille. Si l'humidité est excessive, ce sont les étiquettes qui peuvent se détériorer rapidement. Pour éviter cela, sachez qu'il existe des films transparents électrostatiques qui permettent de protéger les capsules et les étiquettes.

• **Privilégiez la pénombre.** À l'instar du vin, il est conseillé d'entreposer les bouteilles dans un endroit sombre. Privilégiez les ampoules de faible intensité et évitez tout néon. La lumière directe du soleil est particulièrement préjudiciable. Il existe une manière simple et efficace de protéger ses whiskies : gardez-les dans leurs boîtes ou dans leurs coffrets d'origine, qui sont souvent très esthétiques. Dans le cas de bouteilles de collection, vos whiskies n'en garderont que plus de valeur, notamment auprès des responsables de salles des ventes ou de sites de ventes aux enchères.

On affirme généralement qu'une fois mis en bouteille, les spiritueux comme le whisky ne vieillissent plus. Ce n'est pas totalement vrai : de nombreux spécialistes sont persuadés qu'au fil du temps, un échange s'opère à travers le bouchon avec l'air ambiant. Selon ces experts, cela permet une micro-oxygénation salutaire, qui va concourir à façonner et à affiner la palette aromatique et gustative tout en rendant le toucher de bouche plus délicat.

Dernier petit conseil : si vous vous faîtes construire un

HOW TO KEEP A BOTTLE ONCE OPENED

Unlike wine, it is rare that a whole bottle of whisky is drunk in one sitting. In fact, several months—sometimes even several years—can pass before it is finished. Special care must be taken once the level of the whisky in the bottle gets down to the final third, because at that point it becomes highly oxygenated. I strongly advise pouring the contents into a smaller bottle to prevent it from becoming dull and losing its taste and aromas.

In the shorter term, note that certain quality bottles evolve significantly in the weeks after opening and may have a splendid surprise or two in store.

HOW TO TASTE WHISKY

Opening the bottle

Uncorking a bottle of recently produced whisky presents no particular problems. Things are less straightforward with collection whiskies bottled in the 1970s, 1960s, or even 1950s, however, which of course include many iconic expressions prized by connoisseurs. If you are lucky enough to be opening such a prize, proceed with the utmost caution because the cork can often be stuck inside the neck and may break if you are not careful. The secret lies in tilting the bottle slightly to moisten the cork. It should then be twisted a tiny bit, first in one direction and then in the other, in order to loosen it, before you incline the bottle and start the process all over again. The operation requires singular patience, but the rewards make it well worth the effort.

meuble sur mesure, il est impératif de prévoir des étagères modulables et surtout suffisamment larges, car les tailles et les formes des bouteilles sont très hétérogènes.

COMMENT CONSERVER SES BOUTEILLES ENTAMÉES ?

À la différence du vin, quand on ouvre une bouteille de whisky, il est rare qu'elle soit bue le soir même. Il peut s'écouler plusieurs mois, parfois plusieurs années avant qu'elle ne soit vidée. Aussi, convient-il d'être vigilant dès que le niveau du liquide atteint le dernier tiers de la bouteille, car le whisky est alors soumis à une très grande oxygénation. Je vous conseille vivement de transvaser celui-ci dans un flacon au volume inférieur, afin d'éviter qu'il ne s'émousse et perde ses qualités olfactives et gustatives. À moins longue échéance, sachez que certaines belles bouteilles évoluent de façon significative de semaine en semaine après leur ouverture et peuvent vous réserver de magnifiques surprises.

COMMENT DÉGUSTER SES WHISKIES ?

L'ouverture de la bouteille

L'ouverture ne pose aucun problème pour les productions récentes. Mais elle requiert une attention particulière pour les whiskies de collection embouteillés dans les années 1970, 1960 voire 1950, parmi lesquels on retrouve de nombreuses expressions cultes particulièrement prisées des amateurs avertis. Si vous avez la chance d'ouvrir un tel flacon, faites preuve d'une grande délicatesse, car il arrive souvent que le bouchon se soit littéralement collé aux parois et se casse si l'on n'y prend pas garde.

Le secret consiste à incliner la bouteille afin d'imbiber le bouchon. Appliquez ensuite un effort de ro-

OFFICIAL AND INDEPENDENT BOTTLERS

So-called "official" whisky is produced, aged, and bottled by the distillery. These are the products best known to the general public. An independent bottler, on the other hand, buys what he sees as promising casks from the distillery and ages them as he sees fit in a warehouse before bottling them, thus adding his own personal touch to the end product.

Unlike with wine, for which estate bottling is generally recommended, in the whisky world, official and independent bottlers happily rub shoulders.

As an example, independent versions of the single malt Caol Ila (pronounced "coo-eela") are generally more sought after than official ones. Since the 1990s, La Maison du Whisky has marketed more than 350 versions from this brand. Nearly twenty years ago, in the golden age of single malt, the majority of the great names in whisky opened the doors of their warehouses to independent bottlers, from Balvenie and Springbank to Lagavulin and Glendronach. Today, independent bottlers are experiencing a difficult time: in spite of growing interest from whisky lovers, they suffer from very limited access to distilleries, which are increasingly intent on preserving exclusive rights over production. And yet the largest among them—with Gordon & MacPhail and Signatory Vintage in the vanguard—possess in their warehouses some veritable treasures from the halcyon days.

tation millimétrique dans un sens, puis dans l'autre, afin de tenter de desceller le liège, puis inclinez à nouveau la bouteille, avant de recommencer. L'opération nécessite de faire preuve de beaucoup de patience, mais le jeu en vaut la chandelle !

EMBOUTEILLAGES OFFICIELS ET INDÉPENDANTS

Le whisky dit «officiel» est produit, vieilli et embouteillé par une distillerie. Il s'agit des références les plus connues du grand public. Un embouteilleur indépendant achète auprès d'une distillerie des fûts qu'il trouve prometteurs. Il les fait vieillir à sa convenance dans ses chais avant de les mettre en bouteille, imprimant ainsi sa propre touche au produit final.

À la différence du vin, où la mise en bouteille au domaine est généralement recommandée, les embouteillages officiels et indépendants cohabitent en bonne intelligence dans l'univers du whisky.

À titre d'exemple, Caol Ila (qui se prononce «cou laïla») est l'un des single malts dont les versions de négoce sont généralement plus recherchées que les embouteillages officiels. La Maison du Whisky en a d'ailleurs commercialisé plus de 350 depuis les années 1990 !

Il y a près de vingt ans, durant l'âge d'or du single malt, la plupart des grands noms du whisky ouvraient les portes de leurs chais aux embouteilleurs indépendants. De Balvenie à Springbank, en passant par Lagavulin ou Glendronach. Aujourd'hui, le négoce connaît une ère paradoxale : malgré un intérêt croissant de la part des amateurs, il souffre d'un accès très limité aux distilleries (celles-ci se réservent en effet de plus en plus l'exclusivité de leur production). Mais les plus importants d'entre eux, Gordon & MacPhail et Signatory Vintage en tête, possèdent encore de véritables pépites datant de la grande époque.

TASTING

Tradition dictates that a tasting should take place in a neutral environment, so as not to disturb the perception of flavors, aromas, colors, and even the sound of the whisky. The place chosen should be quiet and neither too warm nor too cold, and care should be taken to avoid the presence of unwelcome odors (cooking smells, fragrant flowers, cigar or cigarette smoke, heady perfumes, etc.). Still, you are, of course, free to opt for a more pleasure-seeking approach that leaves more to chance. In any event, the atmosphere of the tasting will be more convivial if you see to it that any potentially intrusive sounds and sights are banished. This is a time to go offline, so turn off your screens and cellphones.

WHAT KIND OF GLASS?

Preferences vary, obviously, but one thing is sure: a good whisky should be tasted in a narrow-necked glass. Unlike a wide-diameter tumbler (which should be kept solely for cocktails), a tulip shape helps to concentrate the vapor and the aromas, thereby enhancing the flavor. Note, too, that it is preferable to use a glass with a foot or base by which to hold it, because touching the sides of the glass will warm the contents, which can alter the whisky's flavor and texture.

AERATION

Although the effect of oxygenation on whisky is less spectacular than in the case of wine, it is nevertheless important to aerate it so as to expand its aromatic range. This is particularly true for cask-strength

LA DÉGUSTATION

Dans la tradition classique, la dégustation doit se dérouler dans un environnement neutre, qui ne risquera pas de perturber la perception des arômes, des saveurs, des couleurs, voire des sons. Privilégiez un lieu calme et tempéré et veillez à éviter la présence d'odeurs ou de parfums importuns (effluves de cuisine, fleurs trop odorantes, fumée de cigares ou de cigarettes, fragrances trop capiteuses, etc.). Mais vous êtes naturellement libre d'opter pour une approche plus hédoniste et laissant plus de place au hasard des circonstances. Quoi qu'il en soit, l'atmosphère de la dégustation ne sera que plus conviviale si vous en profitez pour bannir les sources de nuisances sonores et visuelles. C'est le moment de se déconnecter des écrans et d'éteindre les portables !

QUEL VERRE ?

Les préférences peuvent évidemment varier, mais une chose est certaine : un bon whisky doit être dégusté dans un verre au col resserré. Contrairement au col droit de large diamètre d'un tumbler (à réserver aux cocktails), un col resserré facilitera l'appréciation des arômes en concentrant les vapeurs et les parfums. Notons aussi que la présence d'un pied ou d'une base pour tenir le verre est préférable, car le contact des doigts sur ses parois en réchauffe le contenu, ce qui peut dénaturer ses arômes et sa texture.

L'AÉRATION

Bien que l'effet de l'oxygénation reste moins spectaculaire que dans le cas du vin, sachez qu'il est important d'aérer un whisky pour en ouvrir la palette aroma-

whiskies, with their high alcohol content, which will gain in richness and subtlety by being allowed to breathe for a few minutes.

A carafe, in addition to the visual pleasure it provides, may offer an additional benefit by aerating the contents, in particular with cask-strength whiskies and very old vintages that may have oxidized with the passing years, though it often proves less advantageous for certain young whiskies with a less marked personality. Lastly, do not forget to note the changes affecting the bottles you open: this is the only real way to get to know your cellar well. Which is, after all, the purpose of this book.

WITH WATER OR ICE?

There is an old tradition during tasting sessions that consists in alternating a straight single malt with the same whisky diluted with a little mineral water. This practice is particularly advisable when the alcohol content of the whisky threatens to overpower its subtler flavors. A dose of water may then bring out certain aromas. Start with a few drops and then taste. Continue until you find the right balance, which is something that depends solely on your palate.

As for ice, without wishing to cast aspersions on those who like their whisky chilled or who enjoy *mizuwari*, you should be advised that ice causes a thermal shock that undeniably stifles a whisky's aromas. Admittedly, the whisky will go down all the more easily, because the ice attenuates the effect of the alcohol, but some of the whisky's secrets will remain hidden, which is unfortunate at a tasting session.

tique. C'est particulièrement vrai pour les whiskies bruts de fût, affichant un taux d'alcool élevé, qui gagneront en richesse et en subtilité après quelques minutes d'aération. Outre le plaisir visuel qu'elle procure, une carafe peut avoir un effet bénéfique en permettant une lente aération, notamment sur les whiskies bruts de fût et les très vieux millésimes déjà oxydés au fil des années, alors qu'elle sera moins indiquée pour certains whiskies plus jeunes à la personnalité moins affirmée. Enfin, n'hésitez pas à suivre l'évolution de vos bouteilles ouvertes au fil du temps : c'est le seul moyen de bien connaître sa cave, ce qui est d'ailleurs tout le propos du livre que vous avez entre les mains.

EAU OU GLAÇONS ?

Il existe une ancienne tradition qui consiste à déguster, en alternance, un single malt pur ou allongé d'un peu d'eau minérale. Cette pratique est particulièrement justifiée lorsque la teneur alcoolique du whisky est telle qu'elle masque certaines saveurs plus subtiles. L'eau saura parfois révéler certains arômes. Commencez par quelques gouttes, puis dégustez. Continuez alors jusqu'à atteindre l'équilibre recherché, qui ne dépend que de votre propre palais.

Quant aux glaçons, sans jeter l'opprobre sur les inconditionnels des whiskies très frais et autres mizuwari, sachez qu'ils provoquent toujours un choc thermique et un indéniable repli sur soi des arômes. Certes, le whisky se boira plus facilement, l'effet de l'alcool étant atténué, mais il ne livrera plus tous ses secrets, ce qui est toujours regrettable pour une séance de dégustation...

THE FIVE SENSES OF TASTING

1. Hearing | Sound comes into play less during the tasting itself than when the tasters are settling in. The clink of glasses and bottles, along with the sounds of corks being pulled and whisky being poured into the glass, are like the first notes of an overture starting up before the curtain rises.

2. Sight | Any encounter with a whisky begins with the sense of sight. If you are dealing with a whisky free of coloring agents, its appearance will inform you about its aging. While not an immutable rule, a pale color often heralds a relatively young whisky, while a darker hue suggests significant interaction between the whisky and the oak, in sherry casks particularly. But, as with

LES CINQ SENS DE LA DÉGUSTATION

1. L'ouïe | L'ouïe relève moins de la dégustation à proprement parler que de la mise en condition des dégustateurs. Le clinquement des verres et des bouteilles, les sons de l'ouverture du bouchon et de l'écoulement du whisky versé dans les verres sont comme les trois coups frappés avant une représentation théâtrale.

2. La vue | La rencontre du whisky commence par la vue. Si vous avez affaire à un whisky sans colorants, la vue vous instruira sur son vieillissement. N'en tirez aucune conclusion catégorique, mais une couleur pâle signale souvent un whisky plutôt jeune, tandis qu'une teinte plus foncée suggère plutôt une

sound, appreciating a whisky's tint also serves as a preamble to the pleasure it will procure when tasted: it is an initial facet of its personality.

3. Smell | The sense of smell is primordial during any tasting. It is essential to actively develop it and to learn to distinguish the various components of a whisky's aromatic palette. First of all, breathe in the initial aromas as they emerge from the bottle immediately after it is opened, because, like the primary aromas of a wine, they tend to be fleeting and can disappear almost instantaneously on contact with the air. Be careful, however, not to take a great sniff of the whisky, as its alcohol content can overwhelm the sinuses and leave you reeling.

Once the whisky is poured, you should adopt a gradual, step-by-step approach. Take your time and let it open up. In the case of cask-strength whiskies, it is customary to hold the glass some distance away from your nose in order to smell the liquid, at about rib level, and to approach it slowly to appreciate it.

The sign of a great whisky is that it presents a broad range of aromas over time. In some cases, enjoying a whisky's remarkable nose can delay the moment of tasting, perhaps out of fear that it may not be as good once in the mouth!

The nose is the gateway to understanding a whisky. Identifying its primary aromas goes beyond mere perception: it opens a vast vista of possibilities that lead to all the flavors that follow. It is an invitation to travel further.

Lastly, the sense of smell can also take us back to our childhood. I have observed that even whisky lovers who are not so keen on this phase of tasting can sometimes be consumed by an intense inner joy, a moment of profound connection. I had

interaction importante du whisky et du chêne, en particulier dans des fûts de sherry. Mais comme pour l'ouïe, l'appréciation des teintes est aussi un préambule au plaisir que procurera le whisky lui-même, une première facette de sa personnalité.

3. L'odorat | L'odorat est l'un des sens les plus sollicités lors de la dégustation. Il est essentiel de l'entraîner pour apprendre à distinguer les différents arômes entrant dans la palette aromatique d'un whisky. Songez tout d'abord à cueillir les premiers arômes de la bouteille dès son ouverture, car, comme les parfums primaires du vin, ils peuvent être fugaces et disparaître presque instantanément sous l'effet de l'oxygène. Attention, cependant, à ne pas respirer à pleins poumons un whisky dont la teneur alcoolique vous brûlerait les sinus.

Une fois le whisky versé, adoptez une approche progressive. Prenez votre temps, et laissez-le se révéler. Dans le cas des bruts de fûts, il est d'usage de sentir le liquide en gardant le verre à distance de votre nez, au niveau des côtes, et de l'approcher lentement pour l'apprécier.

Le propre d'un grand whisky est de proposer des arômes différents sur la durée. Dans certains cas, un nez remarquable peut d'ailleurs retarder le moment de la dégustation en elle-même, tant on redoute que la bouche ne soit pas au niveau !

Le nez est la porte d'entrée qui permet de comprendre un whisky. Identifier un premier arôme va au-delà de la simple perception : cela ouvre le champ des possibles, de toutes saveurs qui peuvent en découler. C'est une invitation au voyage. Enfin, l'odorat nous connecte à notre enfance, et j'ai pu observer que même les amateurs de whisky qui ne sont pas passionnés par cette phase de la dégustation peuvent parfois ressentir une intense joie intérieure, un moment de communication viscérale. J'ai eu l'occasion

the opportunity to experience this myself one day with an old Irish whiskey, a Redbreast 25 Year Old, in which I recognized the grassy smell of blackcurrant strigs from my childhood.

4. Touch | A whisky's texture in the mouth is part of the tasting experience. Mouthfeel constitutes the first tactile contact. Thus, a more or less viscous texture contributes in a different way to the pleasures of tasting, unquestionably affecting length.

5. Taste | The sense of taste completes and hones the nose of a whisky, exploiting the more restricted range of sweet, sour, salty, and bitter flavors, as well as umami (i.e., the Japanese word for savory, which describes a fifth taste type that is found, for example, in mushrooms, meat, or fermented food). Note that the act of swallowing can bring out the expression of certain notes in a whisky, such as peatiness, as well as hints of oak and certain spices, due to what is called "retronasal olfaction"—a second wave of aromas that reaches the nose along the interior pathways.

Tasting is, above all, a question of personality. Some whisky buffs learn every subdivision of the flavor wheel by heart and spend their time classifying (and reclassifying) their bottles into families and categories. Others are more readily guided by instinct or curiosity. The purely analytical approach is entirely valid, but it can be intimidating for certain enthusiasts. During master classes, I occasionally encounter people with extraordinary palates who are hesitant to express themselves and to reveal their skills because they do not recognize the same savors as other participants.

Tasting is an intensely individual matter. Each occasion brings with it the opportunity to rediscover your tastes. The complexity of a whisky is like a

de le vivre moi-même en retrouvant dans un vieux whiskey irlandais, le Redbreast de 25 ans, les arômes herbacés des branches de cassis de mon enfance.

4. Le toucher | La dégustation, c'est aussi la sensation d'une texture en bouche. Cette sensation constitue le premier contact tactile. Ainsi, une texture plus ou moins huileuse contribue de manière différente au plaisir de la dégustation et joue indéniablement sur la longueur en bouche.

5. Le goût | Le goût complète et précise le nez d'un whisky en jouant sur la gamme plus restreinte du sucré, de l'acide, du salé, de l'amer et de l'umami (mot japonais signifiant « goût savoureux » et désignant un cinquième goût que l'on retrouve notamment dans les champignons, les viandes ou les aliments fermentés). Sachez que le fait d'avaler peut favoriser l'expression de certaines saveurs du whisky, comme la tourbe, les notes de chêne ou d'épices, en raison de la « rétro-olfaction », deuxième lecture des arômes atteignant le nez par les voies intérieures.

La dégustation est avant tout une affaire de personnalité. Certains passionnés apprennent par cœur chaque sous-division de la roue des arômes et s'efforcent de classer et de reclasser leurs bouteilles par familles et par catégories. D'autres se laissent plus volontiers guider par leur instinct, leur curiosité.

L'approche purement analytique est tout à fait valable, mais elle tend souvent à intimider certains amateurs. Je repère ainsi régulièrement, lors de masterclasses, des personnes aux palais extraordinaires qui tardent à s'exprimer et à révéler leurs capacités, car elles ne reconnaissent pas les mêmes saveurs que les autres.

N'oublions pas que la dégustation est une affaire personnelle et intime. C'est à chaque fois l'occasion de partir à la rencontre de vos propres goûts. La complexité d'un whisky est un labyrinthe où vous pouvez

labyrinth in which you can lose yourself delightfully before pursuing your explorations and picking up the golden thread of all the aromas and flavors that have left their mark on your life.

I hope that you will make this book your own. The following chapter will immerse you in the genesis of whisky, a drink forged over the centuries that has evolved in the light of great historical events. Alcohol possesses the virtue of preserving whatever it contains, and if you are attentive enough, or simply give your imagination free rein as you swirl your glass, you will perhaps be able to detect the scents of the different eras through which that whisky has lived. If you manage to do this, treasure these impressions and note them down in this journal.

At the end of the book, you will find a guide to the best whisky distilleries and an account of their most iconic expressions—in short, another facet of history.

I wish you the greatest pleasure reading, writing, rereading, and of course tasting—because, in the end, that's what it is all about.

Jean-Marc Bellier, store manager
La Maison du Whisky, Paris

prendre plaisir à vous perdre pour mieux retrouver, au hasard de votre exploration, le fil des parfums et saveurs qui ont marqué votre vie.

Il me reste à vous souhaiter de vous approprier ce livre. Dans le chapitre qui suit, vous pourrez vous plonger dans la genèse du whisky, qui s'est forgé au fil des siècles, évoluant au gré des grands événements historique. L'alcool a la vertu de conserver ce qu'il contient, et si vous êtes attentifs, ou laissez simplement à votre imagination assez de liberté, vous pourrez peut-être déceler au détour d'un verre les différents parfums des époques qu'il a traversé. Si tel est le cas, retenez ces impressions et notez-les dans ce livre.

À la fin de l'ouvrage, vous trouverez un guide des meilleures distilleries de whisky et leurs expressions les plus mythiques. Une autre forme d'histoire en somme !

J'espère que vous aurez énormément de plaisir à lire, à écrire, à relire et à déguster, car au fond, il ne s'agit que de cela.

Jean-Marc Bellier, responsable de la boutique
La Maison du Whisky à Paris

A Whisky Chronology

Chronologie du whisky

Whisky possesses a complex, strong, and challenging identity conveyed through a steadily expanding range of expressions that connoisseurs are always keen to learn about and taste.

The history of whisky—full of inventors, rebels, and explorers—leads us from Ireland and Scotland via the United States to Japan, and on to a growing number of regions around the world.

Key Dates

1494 | First official reference to malt distillation in legal documents in Scotland.

1505 | The Guild of Barber Surgeons of Edinburgh obtained a monopoly over the manufacture of aqua vitae.

1550 | Driven out from their monasteries, Scottish monks disseminated their expertise in distillation throughout Scotland and beyond.

1619 | Foundation of the Berkeley plantation in Virginia, where Captain George Thorpe conducted the earliest experiments in distilling spirits from corn.

1644 | Promulgation in Scotland of the first tax on whisky, a spirit whose history would be checkered by modifications in its tax status.

> *At this time, whisky was primarily distilled by private individuals, to use up a grain surplus or to pay in rent to the landowner. Contraband was also one of the most common ways of expressing hostility to the Sassenach.*

1670 | Foundation of the **first legal distillery** in Scotland, at Ferintosh near Inverness. A century later, it was producing two-thirds of all whisky legally distilled in Scotland: in excess of 100,000 US gallons (4,000 hl).

Le whisky est un produit à l'identité affirmée, complexe et exigeante, dont les expressions multiples ne cessent de s'enrichir et suscitent chez l'amateur une véritable passion d'apprentissage et de découverte. Faisant la part belle aux inventeurs, aux rebelles et aux explorateurs, son histoire nous mène des terres d'Irlande et d'Écosse au Japon, en passant par les États-Unis, sans oublier un nombre croissant de nouveaux terroirs qui émergent à travers la planète.

Grandes dates

1494 | Première référence officielle à la distillation de malt dans des documents officiels écossais.

1505 | La guilde des chirurgiens-barbiers d'Édimbourg obtient le monopole de la fabrication d'eau-de-vie.

1550 | Chassés de leurs monastères, les moines écossais diffusent leurs connaissances en matière de distillation en Écosse et au-delà.

1619 | Fondation de la plantation de Berkeley, en Virginie, où le capitaine George Thorpe mène les premières expériences de distillation d'eau-de-vie à partir de maïs.

1644 | Promulgation du premier impôt sur le whisky en Écosse dont l'histoire sera rythmée par des modifications de statut fiscal.

> *Le whisky est alors essentiellement distillé par des particuliers pour écouler leurs surplus de grain ou payer le loyer au propriétaire, la contrebande est l'une des manières les plus populaires d'exprimer son hostilité au pouvoir anglais.*

1670 | Fondation de Ferintosh, la **première distillerie légale d'Écosse,** près d'Inverness. Un siècle plus tard, elle produira les deux tiers du whisky légalement distillé en Écosse, soit plus de 4 000 hl.

1690 | With England and France at war, Scottish smugglers took advantage of the prohibition on wine and cognac to export whisky to their southern neighbors.

1707 | The English Parliament instructed excise officers to enter Scotland to collect duties and destroy stills when necessary.

1725 | Prime Minister Robert Walpole increased the tax on spirits. The ensuing riots in Glasgow left eleven dead.

1760 | Following a poor harvest, commercial distillation was outlawed and a reward offered for the denunciation of moonshine stills. Many distillers turned prohibition on its head by "denouncing" their own decrepit equipment and renewing it with the reward.

1770 | Foundation of Kilbagie, one of the largest distilleries in the Lowlands.

> To reduce costs, the whiskies of the Lowlands were distilled from wheat and unmalted barley or other grains. The resulting lower-quality whisky was then dispatched to England, where it was redistilled into gin.

1781 | The rivalry between the Highlands (deprived of grain crops) and the Lowlands (a European grain importer) was further stoked by famine. For the first time, the British government prohibited the private production of whisky.

1784 | **The Wash Act** placed the administrative division between the Highlands and the Lowlands on an official footing. Many Scots and Irishmen left for America, settling in Pennsylvania, Maryland, Virginia, or Carolina.

1789 | Baptist pastor Elijah Craig set up a distillery in Fayette County, Kentucky, distilling a whiskey made from corn aged in charred oak barrels. According to legend, this is how he invented bourbon.

1690 | L'Angleterre et la France sont en guerre, les contrebandiers écossais profitent de l'interdiction du vin et du cognac pour exporter leur whisky vers l'Angleterre.

1707 | Le parlement britannique charge des officiers d'accises de se rendre en Écosse pour collecter les taxes ou, le cas échéant, détruire les alambics.

1725 | Le Premier ministre Walpole augmente la taxe sur les eaux-de-vie. Des émeutes à Glasgow font 11 morts.

1760 | Suite aux mauvaises récoltes, la distillation commerciale est interdite. Une récompense est offerte pour la dénonciation des alambics clandestins. De nombreux distillateurs en profitent pour livrer leur matériel vétuste et se rééquiper grâce à la récompense perçue.

1770 | Fondation de Kilbagie, l'une des plus importantes distilleries des Lowlands.

> Pour réduire les coûts, les whiskies des Lowlands sont distillés à l'aide de blé et d'orge non maltée ou d'autres céréales. Ce whisky de moindre qualité est alors envoyé en Angleterre où il est redistillé en gin.

1781 | Une famine attise la rivalité entre Highlands (privées de céréales) et Lowlands (qui importent leur grain d'Europe). Pour la première fois, le gouvernement britannique interdit la production individuelle de whisky.

1784 | Le **Wash Act** officialise la division administrative entre Highlands et Lowlands. De nombreux Écossais et Irlandais partent vers l'Amérique pour s'installer en Pennsylvanie, au Maryland, en Virginie et en Caroline.

1789 | Elijah Craig fonde sa distillerie à Fayette County, dans le Kentucky, où l'on distille un whiskey à partir de maïs vieilli dans des fûts de chêne soumis au brûlage. La légende attribue l'invention du bourbon à ce pasteur baptiste.

The name "bourbon" came either from Bourbon County, in Kentucky, or from Bourbon Street in New Orleans, which both refer to the French royal dynasty.

1791–1794 | The **Whiskey Rebellion** in the United States divided whiskey makers from George Washington, who sought to impose a tax to raise funds for the War of Independence.

1808 | Pulling out of the slave trade, America abolished the duty on whiskey, which would be increasingly drunk in preference to rum.

1809 | As a result of the disastrous harvest, distillation was outlawed throughout Scotland (a ban that would be repeated in 1811, 1813, and 1817).

1816 | The line dividing Scotland into Lowlands and Highlands was removed, duties were reduced, and stills of smaller size were authorized.

1820 | The Duke of Gordon, landlord to George Smith of Glenlivet, made a speech defending the value of Highland whisky in the House of Lords. On a visit to Scotland two years later, **King George IV ordered a dram of an illegal whisky**, Glenlivet.

1823 | The promulgation of the **Excise Act** wrought havoc in the whisky industry.

For the British Crown, the legalization of distillation was a means of stifling Scottish independence and enriching major landowners.

1831 | Aeneas Coffey improved the **column still,** invented by Robert Stein a few years earlier. Continuous distillation was widely adopted for making grain whisky.

These new stills made it possible to produce thirty times more by volume per year than with traditional pot stills. They distilled a mellow, if strong, alcohol that was less rich in aromas.

1860 | As transportation became modernized, the sale of whisky in bottles was legalized.

L'origine de l'appellation « bourbon » est associée soit au Bourbon County, dans le Kentucky, soit à la Bourbon Street, à la Nouvelle-Orléans, les deux faisant référence à la dynastie royale française.

1791–1794 | La **Whiskey Rebellion,** aux États-Unis, oppose les fabricants de whiskey à George Washington, qui veut les taxer pour payer la Guerre d'indépendance.

1808 | L'Amérique cesse le commerce des esclaves et abolit la taxe sur le whiskey, dont la consommation remplace progressivement celle du rhum.

1809 | La distillation est interdite à travers toute l'Écosse en raison de récoltes désastreuses (cette interdiction se renouvellera en 1811, 1813 et en 1817).

1816 | La ligne départageant l'Écosse entre Lowlands et Highlands est supprimée, les impôts sont réduits et les alambics de taille inférieure sont autorisés.

1820 | Le duc de Gordon, proche de George Smith de Glenlivet, défend la valeur et l'importance du whisky des Highlands dans la chambre des lords. Deux ans plus tard, Georges IV est en visite en Écosse, et **le roi demande à boire un whisky illégal,** le Glenlivet.

1823 | L'**Excise Act** bouleverse l'industrie du whisky.

Pour la Couronne britannique, la légalisation de la distillation est un moyen de lutter contre les visées indépendantistes écossaises en enrichissant les grands propriétaires terriens.

1831 | Aeneas Coffey perfectionne l'**alambic à colonnes** inventé quelques années plus tôt par Robert Stein. La distillation en continu sera largement adoptée pour le whisky de grain.

Ces nouveaux alambics permettent d'obtenir 30 fois les volumes produits à l'année par les alambics traditionnels pot still. Ils distillent un alcool suave, fortement titré, mais moins riche en parfums.

1860 | Les transports se modernisent et il devient légal de vendre du whisky en bouteille.

1865 | The Cognac region was devastated by **phylloxera**. Deprived of brandy, the English increased their consumption of whisky.

1872 | A trading mission introduced whisky to Japan, in the form of Old Parr.

1909 | A British Royal Commission defined the **official composition of whisky,** including, along with malts, spirits made from other grains and blends.

1915 | The **Immature Spirits Act** introduced compulsory bonding for a period of two years, subsequently extended to three.

1918 | Masataka Taketsuru came from Japan to Scotland to learn how to distill whisky.

1920 | The manufacture, transport, import, export, and sale of alcoholic beverages were made illegal in the United States. **Prohibition** would last thirteen years.

> *Whereas the Irish tended to refuse dealings with smugglers, the Scots appeared less scrupulous, transiting their production via Bermuda, the Bahamas, Cuba, and Canada, where smugglers conveyed the contraband to the coast of America.*

1923 | **Japan founded its first distillery,** Yamazaki.

1933 | Prohibition came to an end in the United States. A new law defined Scotch whisky, imposing a minimum aging period of three years.

1964 | The US Congress issued a resolution recognizing bourbon as a "distinctive product" of the United States.

1980 | The Irish Whiskey Act regulated the methods and techniques of making the Irish product.

2001 | For the first time in history, a Japanese whisky—Yoichi 10-year-old, single-cask—won the prize for best whisky at an international event, the World Whisky Awards.

2009 | The United Kingdom issued the **Scotch Whisky Regulations,** which replaced the preceding

1865 | Le **phylloxéra** sévit dans la région de Cognac. Privés de brandy, les Anglais augmentent leurs importations de whisky.

1872 | Une mission commerciale introduit le premier whisky sur le sol du Japon, le Old Parr.

1909 | Une commission royale britannique définit la **composition officielle du whisky,** et inclut, au côté des malts, les eaux-de-vie d'autres céréales (whisky de grain) et les blends.

1915 | L'**Immature Act** impose une période de garde de 2 ans, qui passera ensuite à 3 ans.

1918 | Masataka Taketsuru arrive en Écosse pour apprendre la fabrication du whisky.

1920 | La fabrication, le transport, l'importation, l'exportation et la vente de boissons alcoolisées sont interdits aux États-Unis. La **Prohibition** durera 13 ans.

> *Alors que les Irlandais refusent de faire affaire avec les contrebandiers, les Écossais, qui ne partagent pas leurs scrupules, font transiter leur production via les Bermudes, les Bahamas, Cuba et le Canada où la marchandise est prise en charge par des contrebandiers pour trouver le chemin des côtes américaines.*

1923 | **Le Japon fonde sa première distillerie,** Yamazaki.

1933 | La Prohibition prend fin aux États-Unis. Une nouvelle loi définit le Scotch Whisky et impose un vieillissement minimum de 3 ans.

1964 | Le Congrès américain promulgue une résolution reconnaissant le bourbon comme une appellation réservée aux États-Unis.

1980 | L'Irish Whiskey Act réglemente les méthodes et techniques de production du whiskey irlandais.

2001 | Pour la première fois dans l'histoire, un whisky japonais, le Yoichi 10 ans single cask, remporte le titre de meilleur whisky dans un événement international, le World Whisky Awards.

regulations of 1988 and 1990. Since 2012, all whiskies termed "single malt Scotch whisky" must be **bottled in Scotland.**

2011 | The term "blended malt" replaced those of "pure malt" and "vatted malt" to designate blends of several single malts.

2015 | For the first time, **a Taiwanese whisky**—Kavalan Solist Vinho Barrique Cask Strength—was **declared the best single malt in the world.**

2009 | La Grande Bretagne promulgue les **Scotch Whisky Regulations,** qui remplacent les réglementations précédentes de 1988 et 1990. À compter de 2012, tout Single Malt Scotch Whisky doit être **mis en bouteille en Écosse.**

2011 | L'appellation Blended Malt remplace les appellations Pure Malt et Vatted Malt pour désigner des assemblages de plusieurs Single Malt.

2015 | Pour la première fois, **un whisky taïwanais,** le Kavalan Solist Vinho Barrique Cask Strength, est **déclaré meilleur single malt au monde.**

A Whisky History

Histoire du whisky

I | Origins

A CONTESTED HISTORY

Ireland and Scotland have long been at loggerheads with regards to the origin of whisky. In fact, depending on the question that is being asked, both countries could legitimately claim to have invented the spirit. But most historians are in agreement that Ireland was the first country to have distilled aqua vitae from barley.

During the turmoil that gripped the rest of Europe in the fifth century, Ireland enjoyed relative peace and quiet, attracting scholars and experts from every walk of life. Saint Patrick himself reportedly introduced the technique of distillation in 432. Later testimony from English soldiers in the twelfth century described monasteries distilling spirits in the country.

Yet it was in Scotland that whisky seems to have acquired the fundamental characteristics by which it is known today.

The first written evidence of the production of spirits from malt in that country dates back to 1494. As a result, an obscure Tironensian monk and apothecary at Lindores Abbey, Brother John Cor, became a famous figure in the history of whisky, since the Exchequer Rolls attest that he was granted an order from King James IV of Scotland to deliver some seventeen hundredweight of malt on June 1, 1495 in order to produce aqua vitae. Such a quantity leads one to believe that whisky production and consumption were by then already entrenched in Scotland.

I | Les origines

UNE NAISSANCE DISPUTÉE

Un vieux débat oppose l'Irlande et l'Écosse sur l'origine du whisky, mais les deux hypothèses sont pertinentes, selon la question posée. Si l'on s'intéresse au premier pays ayant pratiqué la distillation d'eau-de-vie à partir d'orge, l'Irlande semble désignée par la majorité des historiens.

En effet, dans les tourments endurés par l'Europe au ve siècle, l'Irlande connaissait une relative quiétude qui exerçait une certaine attraction sur les détenteurs de savoirs provenant de tous horizons. Le célèbre Saint Patrick y aurait ainsi introduit la technique de la distillation dès 432. On dispose d'ailleurs de témoignages de soldats anglais datant du xiie siècle où sont décrits des monastères distillant de l'eau-de-vie.

Mais c'est bien sur les terres d'Écosse que le whisky semble avoir trouvé l'identité fondamentale sous laquelle nous le connaissons actuellement.

La première trace écrite attestant de la production d'eau-de-vie à partir de malt en Écosse remonte à 1494. C'est à elle qu'un obscur moine tironien et apothicaire de l'abbaye de Lindores, le frère John Cor, doit d'être devenu une figure célèbre de l'histoire du whisky. Des documents nationaux attestent en effet qu'il a bénéficié d'un ordre du roi James IV d'Écosse pour se faire livrer, le 1er juin 1495, près de 900 kg de malt afin de produire de l'eau-de-vie. Une telle quantité laisse supposer que la production et la consommation de whisky étaient alors des pratiques bien établies en Écosse.

Every collector is by nature a traveler, and there can be no better excuse for venturing abroad than a pilgrimage: to Lindores Abbey, for instance, located little more than an hour by road from Edinburgh, today considered by many respected specialists as the "birthplace of whisky."

EARLY DISTILLATION

To distill a liquid is to extract and purify its lightest, finest, and most aromatic fractions—or, quoting Rabelais's celebrated expression, to "abstract its quintessence." Applied to an ale brewed from barley (before the addition of hops) or other grains, this "abstraction" produces a spirit that, once aged, is called whisky.

The origins of distillation are lost in the mists of time, though the process was described in the third century by alchemists such as Zosimos of Panopolis, who in one of his works describes a still observed in the Egyptian city of Memphis. Europe's earliest distillers may have been inspired by the work of Arab philosopher and astronomer Jabir ibn Hayyan, the founder of modern chemistry, who died at the beginning of the ninth century and who drew the earliest-known diagrams of a still employed to obtain acids such as aqua regia. The making of "burning water," i.e., alcohol, was perfected from the thirteenth century in Salerno in southern Italy.

"WHISKY" BEFORE WHISKY

It should not be forgotten that, at a time when the sole means of preserving food was to macerate it in salt or to ferment it, the power of alcohol to remain unspoiled for years has something of a supernatural dimension to it.

Tout collectionneur est un voyageur dans l'âme, et quelle meilleure excuse pour un voyage qu'un pèlerinage ? Aujourd'hui, l'abbaye de Lindores, située à un peu plus d'une heure de route d'Édimbourg, est considérée par certains grands spécialistes comme le lieu de naissance du whisky.

LES ORIGINES DE LA DISTILLATION

Distiller un liquide, c'est en extraire et en purifier la part la plus délicate, la plus légère et la plus aromatique : en « abstraire la quintessence », pour reprendre la célèbre expression de Rabelais. Appliquée à une bière d'orge (avant toute adjonction de houblon) ou d'autres céréales, cette abstraction produit une eau-de-vie qui, après vieillissement, sera appelée whisky.

Les origines de la distillation sont anciennes et décrites dès le IIIe siècle par des alchimistes comme Zosime le Panopolitain, qui, dans ses œuvres, décrit un alambic observé dans la cité égyptienne de Memphis. Les premiers distillateurs européens ont pu s'inspirer des travaux de l'Arabe Jabir ibn Hayyan, philosophe, astronome et fondateur de la chimie moderne mort au début du IXe siècle, auteur des premiers diagrammes d'alambics connus, alors utilisés pour obtenir des acides comme l'eau royale. La fabrication d'« eau ardente », c'est-à-dire d'alcool, est perfectionnée à partir du XIIIe siècle à Salerne, au sud de l'Italie.

LE WHISKY AVANT LE WHISKY

Il ne faut pas oublier que la capacité qu'a l'alcool de ne pas se dénaturer au fil des années avait une dimension véritablement surnaturelle à une époque où le seul moyen de conserver la nourriture consistait à la faire macérer dans le sel ou la faire fermenter.

The origin of the expression "aqua vitae" reflects the idea of the elixir of life—that is, a concoction capable of cleansing wounds, alleviating pain (dental, in particular), calming tremors, and curing stomach cramp. It could also be rubbed onto the forehead to relieve a headache. One sixteenth-century physician believed that moderate consumption could drive out melancholia, reduce the occurrence of kidney stones, improve diction, and clear the sinuses. These same beneficial virtues were to be extolled for alcohol many centuries later in the United States, during Prohibition.

FOR HEALTH, BUT FOR PLEASURE TOO

In a tome from 1527, Scottish historian Hector Boece describes a spirit designed to be drunk for reasons other than medicinal ones that was "devoid of any spice and containing only grasses and roots that grow in their gardens." This meant, in all probability, local plants such as thyme, rosemary, sorbus, and heather, with the possible addition of lavender, marjoram, hyssop, and heather honey.

A *SKALK* FIRST THING IN THE MORNING

If one is to believe Dr. Samuel Johnson's travel journal, the **skalk** was a common practice in the Hebrides during the late eighteenth century. It consisted of a dram of whisky knocked back before breakfast! Johnson goes on to reassure us that this tradition, if universal among the menfolk, did not at all herald a day of unbridled potation. The famous English linguist nonetheless observes that the word comes from the Scots Gaelic meaning "a whack to the head".

L'origine de l'expression « eau-de-vie » reflète la notion d'élixir de vie, c'est-à-dire d'une concoction capable de nettoyer les plaies, d'alléger les douleurs (en particulier dentaires), de calmer les tremblements, de guérir les crampes d'estomac. On s'en frottait parfois le front pour soulager les maux de tête. Un médecin du XVIe siècle croyait également qu'une consommation modérée pouvait chasser la mélancolie, réduire les calculs rénaux, améliorer la diction et dégager les sinus. Toutes ces vertus bienfaisantes seront remises à l'honneur bien des siècles plus tard aux États-Unis pendant la Prohibition...

POUR LA SANTÉ, MAIS AUSSI POUR LE PLAISIR...

L'historien écossais Hector Boece décrit, dans un ouvrage de 1527, une eau-de-vie destinée à être dégustée sans visées médicales, « dépourvue de toute épice et contenant seulement les herbes et racines qui poussaient dans leurs jardins », c'est-à-dire, en toute vraisemblance, des plantes locales telles que le thym, le romarin, le sorbier et la bruyère, éventuellement additionnés de lavande, de marjolaine, d'hysope et de miel de bruyère.

UN *SKALK* DE BON MATIN

Le **skalk** était une pratique répandue dans les Hébrides écossaises vers la fin du XVIIIe siècle, si l'on en croit les carnets de voyage du Dr Samuel Johnson. Un dram de whisky y était ainsi consommé et offert en guise d'apéritif... avant le petit-déjeuner ! Il est aussitôt précisé que cette tradition, de rigueur pour tous les hommes, ne signalait pas le début de journées placées sous le signe d'une consommation débridée. Le célèbre linguiste anglais précise d'ailleurs que le mot vient du gaélique écossais signifiant « un coup à la tête ».

In this period, whisky was drunk from a "quaich," a decorated, shallow wooden bowl with handles on both sides, which is still associated with various Celtic rituals.

MAKING WHISKY

Ingredients

Just three ingredients suffice to produce the incredible diversity of single malt Scotch: water, a grain (primarily barley), and yeast.

1. **Water**

   Great distilleries consume huge quantities of water and often stand near rivers or lochs. Water is added at the mashing stage and is employed to cool the still's condensers. Sometimes, it can be used to dilute the whisky prior to bottling. Water is the only ingredient in whisky that reflects local characteristics in the technical sense. For example, the spring at Tarlogie provides Glenmorangie with water that is particularly rich in calcium, magnesium, and zinc, which concentrate the flavor during fermentation.

2. **Grains**

   Barley: The most costly item in a distillery's budget, barley is the key ingredient in determining the range of flavors in a whisky. The selection of its varieties is an essential factor in production. Technically speaking, barley has the advantage of being rich in starch and is the grain that guarantees the highest production of enzymes, essential to the breakdown of starch into sugar during malting. In addition, barley is employed to kick-start the fermentation of other grains, such as the wheat that features in many blends.

Le whisky se buvait alors dans un «quaich», sorte de bol en bois décoré peu profond à poignées situées de part et d'autre qui reste associé à certains rituels celtiques.

LA FABRICATION DU WHISKY

Ingrédients

Trois ingrédients suffisent à faire naître l'incroyable diversité des single malts écossais : l'eau, une céréale (en particulier l'orge) et des levures.

1. **Eau**

   Les grandes distilleries se situent souvent à proximité de rivières (ou de lacs), car elles sont de grandes consommatrices d'eau. L'eau est ajoutée lors du brassage, utilisée pour refroidir les condenseurs des alambics et elle intervient parfois pour diluer le whisky avant la mise en bouteille. L'eau est le seul ingrédient du whisky qui reflète une dimension de terroir au sens technique. Par exemple, la source de Tarlogie fournit à Glenmorangie une eau particulièrement riche en calcium, en magnésium et en zinc qui permet de concentrer les arômes pendant la fermentation.

2. **Céréales**

   Orge : l'orge constitue l'un des ingrédients les plus importants, impactant sur la palette aromatique du whisky. C'est d'ailleurs le premier poste de dépense pour une distillerie. La sélection des variétés est essentielle dans la fabrication d'un whisky.

   Sur le plan technique, l'orge a l'avantage d'être riche en amidon et d'être la céréale qui garantit la plus importante production d'enzymes, essentielles pour assurer la dégradation de l'amidon en sucre lors du maltage. L'orge est d'ailleurs utilisée pour

Corn: Used in Scottish grain distilleries until the 1980s, corn is today associated with American whiskeys, in particular with bourbon, in which it always comprises at least 51%, giving this type of whiskey its characteristic roundness and mildness.

Rye: This grain dominates in American and Canadian ryes, a minimum of 51% being the norm in the US, and results in a type of whiskey that is generally drier and fruitier than bourbon.

Wheat: The predominant grain in Scotch blends since the 1980s, it very rarely features in American whiskeys.

3. **Yeast**

These microorganisms transform sugar into alcohol during fermentation. They also enrich the range of its aromas. Though yeast is naturally present in the atmosphere, the yield from such a source tends to be unpredictable, and the majority of major distilleries prefer to culture yeasts whose strains and exact composition are jealously kept trade secrets.

The traditional process

The manufacture of whisky, in its traditional Scottish variant, starts with the **malting** of the barley, by which it is soaked in lukewarm water so as to activate germination and produce enzymes. Germination is then halted by drying with hot air, sometimes produced by burning peat. The malted barley is then ground into a meal (the grist), mixed with water, and heated in mash tuns, where the heat and enzymes transform the barley's starch into sugar in a process known as **mashing.** The wort thus obtained is then conveyed to wooden containers, where it is enriched with yeast to ensure its **fermentation** into wash— a

amorcer la fermentation d'autres céréales comme le blé (utilisé dans de nombreux blends).

Maïs : utilisé dans les distilleries de grain écossaises jusque dans les années 1980, le maïs est aujourd'hui associé aux whiskeys américains, en particulier au bourbon, où il est toujours présent à au moins 51 % et confère une rondeur et une douceur caractéristiques à ce style de whiskey.

Seigle : le seigle domine dans les rye américains et canadiens, où il est présent à hauteur de 51 % au minimum côté US et permet de fabriquer un breuvage généralement plus sec et plus fruité que le bourbon.

Blé : céréale dominante des blends écossais depuis les années 1980, il est très peu utilisé dans les whiskeys américains.

3. **Levures**

Ce sont ces micro-organismes qui transforment le sucre en alcool pendant la fermentation. Ils contribuent également à enrichir sa palette aromatique. Les levures sont naturellement présentes dans l'atmosphère, mais leur rendement peut être aléatoire et la plupart des grandes distilleries leur préfèrent les levures de culture dont les souches et la composition exacte sont des secrets de fabrication jalousement gardés.

Élaboration d'origine

La fabrication du whisky, sous sa version écossaise traditionnelle, commence par le **maltage** de l'orge, qui est trempée dans une eau tiède pour activer sa germination et produire des enzymes. Un séchage à l'air chaud (parfois produit par combustion de tourbe) vient ensuite interrompre cette germination. L'orge maltée est alors réduite en farine (le *grist*), mélangée à de l'eau et chauffée dans des *mash tuns*, où la chaleur et les enzymes transforment l'amidon de l'orge en sucres : c'est

kind of ale of about 7% alcohol. It is this wash that is transferred into the stills to be distilled.

Distillation—a process repeated two or three times, depending on the distillery's particular tradition and the stills employed—is designed to vaporize and then recover the alcohol, together with aromatic congeners in the wash.

DOUBLE VS. TRIPLE DISTILLATION

The method traditionally practiced in the majority of Scotland (except in a number of Lowland distilleries) is double distillation.

Triple distillation is characteristic of Irish whiskey and is designed to produce a lighter single malt dominated by floral and fruity notes.

The art of the distiller consists essentially in identifying and isolating the "heads" and "tails" of the distillation—the terms for, respectively, the liquid obtained at the beginning and at the end of distillation.

The initial fractions are rejected because they contain methanol, while the tails may be marred by undesirable aromatic compounds.

A REVOLUTIONARY STILL

The column still was invented in 1826 by Robert Stein, whose family possessed the Kilbagie distillery, radically transforming whisky production. Instead of having to clean out the still after each batch, it was henceforth possible to continue distilling without interruption, and so produce about thirty times more whisky than using traditional Scottish methods. The alcohol thus obtained is purer, mellower, and of a higher proof, but sometimes less rich in savor.

le **brassage**. Le *wort* ainsi obtenu est transféré vers des conteneurs de bois où il est enrichi de levures pour assurer sa **fermentation** en *wash*, c'est-à-dire une sorte de bière titrant environ 7 ° d'alcool. C'est ce wash qui sera acheminé vers les alambics afin d'être distillé.

La **distillation,** processus répété deux ou trois fois en fonction des traditions et des alambics utilisés, permet de vaporiser puis de récupérer l'alcool et certains éléments aromatiques du wash.

DOUBLE OU TRIPLE DISTILLATION ?

La méthode traditionnellement pratiquée dans la majorité de l'Écosse (hormis certaines distilleries des Lowlands) est la double distillation.

La triple distillation est caractéristique des whiskeys irlandais et permet d'obtenir des single malt plus légers où dominent des notes florales et fruitées.

L'art du distillateur consiste notamment à identifier et à isoler les têtes et les queues de distillation. On appelle ainsi, respectivement, le liquide obtenu en début et en fin de distillation. Les premières vapeurs sont rejetées, car elles contiennent du méthanol, tandis que les queues de distillation sont reconnaissables à leurs composés aromatiques indésirables.

UN ALAMBIC RÉVOLUTIONNAIRE

En 1826, la colonne continue est inventée par Robert Stein, dont la famille détient la distillerie Kilbagie. Ceci modifie fondamentalement la production de whisky. Au lieu d'avoir à nettoyer l'alambic après chaque *batch*, il est désormais possible de distiller en continu et de produire environ 30 fois plus de whisky que selon les méthodes traditionnelles pratiquées au Nord. L'alcool obtenu est plus pur, plus suave, affiche un titre d'al-

That model was soon ousted by another, perfected by the Irishman Aeneas Coffey in Dublin, that was more efficient and less expensive. By 1836, 30% of Lowland distilleries were using a Coffey still.

MATURATION

The colorless spirit obtained through distillation is then aged in casks for a minimum of three years. Aging plays an essential role in the development of a whisky's array of flavors. Vanillin, for example, is an aldehyde with a very pronounced taste that manifests itself right at the beginning of aging through the interaction between the alcohol and the wood. Likewise, it is during the early years of maturation that the wood confers a golden or amber glow on the initially colorless liquid.

Scotch whisky makers prefer older casks, often ones previously used for bourbon or various wines, which have the advantage of creating richer hues and more complex flavors than casks made of new oak.

Aromatic esters take more time to develop. Over the years, a whisky will evolve from a flavor generally dominated by the grains to develop fruitier notes, then, as time passes, more exotic notes that originate in the lactones present in the oak. With the progressive release of glycerol and sugar, the spirit also becomes smoother in texture.

The "angels' share" describes the proportion of the whisky that evaporates from the cask each year as it ages. Varying according to climate and the size of the cask used, it is about 2% in Scotland, rising to 4% or more for whiskey in warehouses in Kentucky and Tennessee.

Being more volatile, the alcohol normally evaporates first, so that proof decreases with time. It can also

cool plus élevé, mais parfois moins riche en saveurs. Ce modèle est bientôt remplacé par celui de l'Irlandais Aeneas Coffey, mis au point à Dublin, plus efficace et moins coûteux. En 1836, 30 % des distilleries des Lowlands utilisent des alambics Coffey still.

LA MATURATION

L'alcool incolore ainsi obtenu est mis à vieillir en fûts pendant un minimum de trois ans. Le vieillissement joue un rôle essentiel dans le développement de la palette aromatique d'un whisky. La «vanilline», par exemple, est un aldéhyde à l'arôme très prononcé apparaissant dès le début du vieillissement du fait de l'interaction entre l'alcool et le bois. C'est également dès les premières années que le bois confère au whisky, initialement incolore, sa teinte dorée ou ambrée.

Les whiskies écossais privilégient les anciens fûts, souvent de bourbon ou de xérès (sherry), qui transmettent au distillat des arômes plus complexes que les fûts de chêne neuf.

Il faut davantage de temps pour développer des esters aromatiques. Au fil des années, les whiskies passent d'arômes généralement dominés par les céréales, pour développer des notes plus fruitées puis, après des durées plus longues, sous l'effet des lactones présentes dans le chêne, des notes plus exotiques. Sa texture devient également de plus en plus suave en raison de la libération progressive de sucres et de glycérols.

*La **part des anges** (ou «angel's share») désigne la proportion de whisky qui s'évapore des fûts chaque année de maturation. Elle varie selon le climat et la taille des fûts utilisés. Elle est de 2 % en Écosse, mais peut s'élever à 4 % ou davantage pour les whiskeys stockés dans les chais du Kentucky ou du Tennessee.*

be the case, however, that warmth combined with low relative humidity increases the evaporation of water, resulting in a higher concentration of alcohol. This is true, for example, of the bourbon Elijah Craig Barrel Proof, barreled at 62.5°, which rises to 68.7° by the time it is bottled.

GROWING CONDITIONS AND WHISKY

The concept of local conditions—the essential terroir in French wine production—tends to be less relevant in the case of whisky. Admittedly, the immense majority of distilleries are intimately bound to their location, but the composition of the soil and local climatic conditions play no real role, since the barley, except in rare cases, is not grown in the vicinity.

WHISKY AND PEAT

A frequent subject of discussion among whisky lovers, peat is first and foremost a natural resource particularly rich in carbon (hence its black color), originating from the decomposition of moss and ferns, that has long been used as a domestic and industrial fuel in the countries of Northern Europe.

Burned in order to dry the barley, it confers an instantly recognizable smoky smell that is often present in whiskies produced on the island of Islay, such as Laphroaig, Lagavulin, and Bruichladdich, for example.

En général, c'est d'abord l'alcool, plus volatil, qui s'évapore le premier, son taux diminuant alors au fil des ans. Mais il peut également arriver que la chaleur alliée à une faible hygrométrie entraîne une évaporation d'eau plus importante et une concentration alcoolique de plus en plus élevée. C'est plus souvent le cas dans la moitié sud États-Unis, comme avec le bourbon Elijah Craig Barrel Proof, par exemple, mis en fût à 62,5° et atteignant 68,7° au moment de sa mise en bouteille.

LES WHISKIES ONT-ILS UN TERROIR ?

Le concept de terroir, essentiel dans l'univers du vin, n'offre pas la même pertinence en ce qui concerne le whisky. Certes, la grande majorité des distilleries sont très attachées à leur région d'origine, mais la composition des sols et le profil climatique locaux ne jouent aucun rôle dans la mesure où l'orge, sauf exception, n'est pas cultivée sur place.

TOURBE ET WHISKY

Sujet récurrent de conversation parmi les amateurs de whisky, la tourbe est à l'origine une ressource naturelle particulièrement riche en carbone (d'où sa couleur noire), provenant de la décomposition des mousses et des fougères, qui a longtemps servi de combustible domestique et industriel dans les pays nordiques.

Son utilisation lors du séchage de l'orge confère au malt un parfum fumé très facilement reconnaissable et souvent présent dans les whiskies produits sur l'île d'Islay, par exemple, comme Laphroaig, Lagavulin ou Bruichladdich.

THE IMPACT OF PPM

The presence of peatiness is measured in "ppm" (parts per million), indicating the concentration of phenol in the malt. Below are some basic figures illustrating the difference between Speyside and Islay whiskies:
- Glenlivet: 2 ppm (a traditional example of an "unpeated" whisky)
- Laphroaig 10 Year Old: 35 ppm (a benchmark)
- Bruichladdich Octomore 07.1: 208 ppm (a record that has its devoted fans)

It is worth noting that phenol concentration, i.e., peatiness, decreases with age (if 10-year-old Laphroaig comes in at 35 ppm, only 6 ppm are left in the 30-year-old whisky).

"UNDILUTED ISLAY"

The island of Islay is considered by many as the global capital of "authentic" whisky. According to a report of 1863, for instance, Glasgow taverns divided their whiskies into four grades of ascending quality: "middling," "good," "Islay," and "undiluted Islay."

L'IMPACT DES PPM

Sa présence peut se mesurer en «ppm» («parts par million»), indiquant la concentration en phénols dans le malt. Voici quelques ordres de grandeur pour illustrer la différence entre un whisky du Speyside et de l'île d'Islay :
- Glenlivet : 2 ppm (un exemple classique de whisky non tourbé).
- Laphroaig 10 ans : 35 ppm (l'une des références incontournables).
- Octomore 07,1 de Bruichladdich : 208 ppm (un record qui a ses inconditionnels).

Sachez que la concentration en phénols, c'est-à-dire en arômes tourbés, diminue au fil de la maturation (le Laphroaig 10 ans d'âge affiche 35 ppm, mais seulement 6 ppm de phénols sont encore présents dans le 30 ans d'âge).

«ISLAY NON DILUÉ»

L'île d'Islay incarne pour beaucoup la capitale mondiale d'un whisky «authentique». À cette enseigne, il est rapporté qu'en 1863, les tavernes de Glasgow classaient leurs whiskies en quatre catégories par ordre croissant de qualité : «médiocre», «bon», «Islay» et «Islay non dilué».

II |
The Adventurous Early Centuries

Whisky in Scotland, Ireland, and the United States: A history marked by smuggling

In eighteenth-century Scotland, only the Lowlands benefited from abundant arable land, while the inhabitants of the Highlands struggled to subsist on their harvests. For farming families, however, the only means of raising the rent money for agricultural land owned by the nobility often consisted in distilling surplus crops.

Problems arose when whisky production began to be practiced on an increasingly large scale, creating food shortages. The State imposed draconian taxes, even totally prohibiting distillation throughout the British Isles for three years after the catastrophic harvests of 1757.

SCOTLAND SPLIT IN TWO

In 1784, the **Wash Act** divided Scotland into two areas along a border running from Greenock in the west to Dundee on the east coast. Each region developed its own distinctive methods of whisky production. While in the north, makers continued to use only malted barley and copper stills of modest dimensions, the south broke with tradition and started mixing malted barley with other grains such as corn, oats, and wheat. The Lowlands thus shifted to industrial production, as in the distilleries of Kilbagie and

II |
L'aventure des premiers siècles

L'histoire du whisky en Écosse, en Irlande et aux États-Unis a longtemps été marquée par la contrebande.

Dans l'Écosse du XVIIIe siècle, seule la région des Lowlands dispose d'abondantes terres arables, tandis que les habitants des Highlands peinent à vivre de leurs propres récoltes. Toutefois, le seul moyen de payer le droit d'exploiter les terres des nobles consistait souvent, pour les familles d'agriculteurs, à distiller leur surplus de récolte.

La difficulté vient du fait que la production de whisky se pratique à échelle de plus en plus grande, ce qui peut entraîner des disettes. L'État impose des politiques fiscales draconiennes qui vont jusqu'à l'interdiction totale de la distillation à travers toutes les îles britanniques pendant les trois années qui suivent les récoltes catastrophiques de 1757.

L'ÉCOSSE SCINDÉE EN DEUX

En 1784, le **Wash Act** divise l'Écosse en deux, selon une frontière tracée de Greenock, à l'Ouest, jusqu'à Dundee, sur la côte Est. Chaque région développe des méthodes de production de whisky distinctes. Tandis que l'on continue d'utiliser uniquement l'orge maltée et des alambics de cuivre de taille modeste au Nord, le Sud s'affranchit de la tradition et associe l'orge maltée à d'autres céréales comme le maïs, l'avoine et le

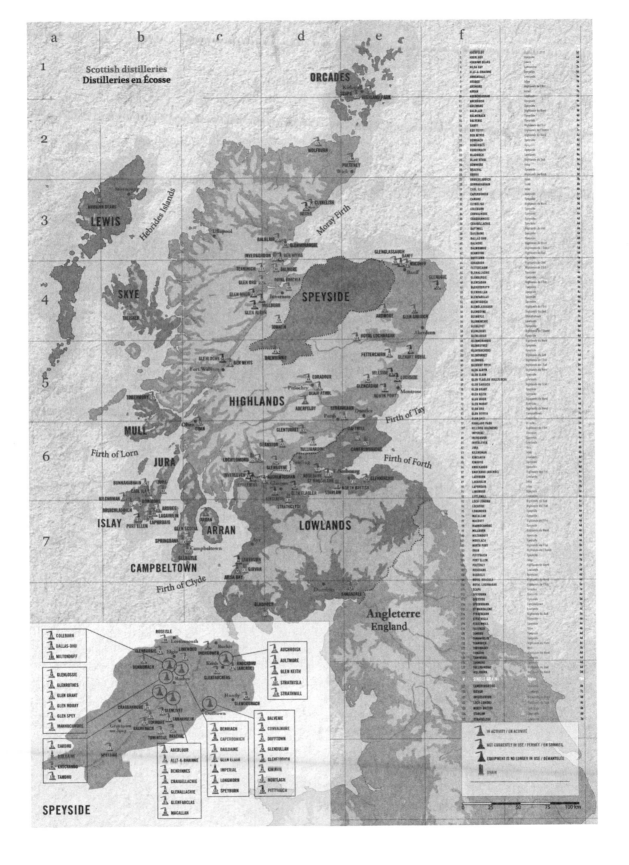

Scottish distilleries
Distilleries en Écosse

Kennetpans, a proportion of whose production was exported to England to be used in the manufacture of gin. This geographical split lasted until 1816.

At one point, the export of the whisky produced on a small scale in the north was simply banned, and the prohibition was extended to include distillation for private consumption from 1778. However, since it enjoyed a superior reputation and proved essential to the economy of the area, smuggling was rife.

THE DECISIVE ELOQUENCE OF THE DUKE OF GORDON

In 1820, the Duke of Gordon sat in the House of Lords, where he pronounced a vigorous speech in defense of Highland whisky. Pleading in favor of a law that would authorize and encourage whisky production, he explained that this would put an end to the issue of smuggling. In particular, the duke referred to the clandestine activities of a distiller of singular talent, a certain George Smith, who would soon take up the reins at Glenlivet, the first distillery to be licensed in Scotland.

Receiving its license in 1608, Bushmills in Ireland was the first legal distillery in the world.

Three years later, the promulgation by Parliament of the Excise Act in 1823 reduced duties on whisky and facilitated its export, thereby revolutionizing the industry in Britain. As long as distillation remained a cottage industry, it was a way of resisting the yoke of the British Crown, but, as capitalism tightened its hold, the former lairds of Scotland, cognizant of the potential of this new source of income, transformed themselves into resourceful landowners.

In the two years following the passing of the law, the number of licensed distilleries doubled, with the

blé. Les Lowlands privilégient dès lors une production industrielle, à l'image des distilleries Killbagie et Kennetpans dont une partie des distillats est exportée en Angleterre pour servir à fabriquer du gin. Cette division durera jusqu'en 1816.

Quant au whisky produit artisanalement au Nord, son exportation est interdite. Dès 1778, cette interdiction s'étend à la distillation privée. Mais comme sa réputation est meilleure et qu'il est indispensable à l'économie de la région, la contrebande fleurit.

L'ÉLOQUENCE DÉCISIVE DU DUC DE GORDON

En 1820, le duc de Gordon se rend à la Chambre des Lords et se livre à une vibrante défense du whisky des Highlands. Il plaide alors pour une législation qui autoriserait et encouragerait la production de whisky, expliquant que cela mettrait fin au problème posé par la contrebande. Il cite notamment l'activité clandestine d'un distillateur de grand talent, un certain George Smith, qui ne tardera pas à diriger la première distillerie écossaise sous licence, à Glenlivet.

Bushmills, en Irlande, reste la première distillerie légale au monde, puisqu'elle a reçu cette licence en 1608.

Trois ans plus tard, en 1823, la promulgation par le parlement britannique de l'Excise Act diminue les taxes et facilite l'exportation, ce qui révolutionne l'industrie du whisky au Royaume-Uni. Tant que la distillation était une activité artisanale, elle était une manière d'échapper au joug de la couronne anglaise, mais avec l'avènement du capitalisme au Royaume-Uni, les anciens seigneurs féodaux écossais se transforment en propriétaires avisés, sensibles au potentiel de cette nouvelle source de revenus.

Deux ans après le passage de la loi, le nombre de distilleries licenciées double. La production légale

production of legally produced whisky soaring from 2.4 to 7.1 million US gallons (9 to 27 million liters) yearly. A total of 337 distilleries emerged from the shadows to acquire their license the following year, in spite of vehement opposition from groups of smugglers. In 1823, there had been no fewer than 14,000 identified clandestine distilleries; by 1834, a mere 692 were left.

NEW WORLD, NEW WHISKEYS

On the other side of the Atlantic, the earliest whiskeys were distilled primarily from rye. Corn began to predominate only from 1774, when an increasing number of colonists settled in Kentucky (then part of the state of Virginia). This fertile region possesses abundant spring water filtered by limestone formations that confer properties much appreciated by brewers and distillers. Rich in calcium, the water is low in iron salts, a combination that promotes yeast activity during fermentation.

Until the end of the nineteenth century, distillation was just one of the farmer's daily tasks, like bread-making or salting food. The whiskey from this period was never aged. A product for everyday consumption, it was an expedient for making money from a corn surplus and offered all the advantages of a parallel currency: easy to store and split up, it also traveled well. In these rural environments, of course, barter played a crucial economic role.

As in Scotland and Ireland, relations between the distillers and the federal tax authorities left much to be desired. In 1791, an insurrection broke out against duties imposed by Washington that were seen as grossly unfair: applied to a distillery's entire potential production, they were calculated not on actual sales but according to the capacity of the stills. This Whiskey Rebellion, however, would soon lose steam.

annuelle de whisky passe de 9 à 27 millions de litres. Un total de 337 distilleries sortent de la clandestinité et prennent une licence dès l'année suivante, malgré un climat d'opposition véhémente entretenu par certains contrebandiers. En 1823, on ne comptait pas moins de 14 000 distilleries clandestines identifiées. En 1834, Il n'en reste que 692.

NOUVEAU MONDE, NOUVEAU WHISKEY

Outre Atlantique, les premiers whiskeys fabriqués utilisent surtout le seigle. Le maïs ne devient dominant qu'à partir de 1774, lorsqu'une population croissante de colons s'installe dans le Kentucky (qui fait alors partie de l'État de Virginie). La région est fertile et abondante en eau de source, filtrée par des formations calcaires qui lui confèrent des propriétés très prisées des brasseurs et des distillateurs (elle est riche en calcium et dépourvue de sels ferreux, ce qui favorise l'action des levures lors de la fermentation).

Jusqu'à la fin du XIXe siècle, la distillation fait partie des tâches courantes de la ferme, au même titre que la fabrication du pain ou les salaisons. Le whiskey de cette période n'est jamais vieilli. C'est un produit de consommation courante qui permet de rentabiliser les excédents de maïs et offre tous les avantages d'une monnaie parallèle : il se conserve, peut se diviser et voyage facilement. Le troc joue en effet un rôle essentiel dans cet environnement économique rural.

Tout comme en Écosse et en Irlande, un climat délétère règne entre les distillateurs et les autorités fiscales fédérales. En 1791, une insurrection éclate contre les taxes exigées par Washington, jugées injustes, car elles portent sur l'intégralité de la production potentielle (elles sont calculées en fonction de la capacité des alambics et non sur les ventes). Mais

When Washington sent an army of 13,000 men to oppose them, the rebels capitulated without a shot being fired: an American Civil War between the coastal states and the Ohio valley region had just been narrowly avoided.

THE LEGENDARY ELIJAH CRAIG

According to folklore, it was the pastor Elijah Craig who invented bourbon. Today, though, all the evidence points to this being a legend concocted by nineteenth-century historians eager to ascribe the paternity of this "unholy" beverage to a man of the cloth.

THE ORIGIN OF THE NAME "BOURBON"

The source of the term bourbon is a real mystery. Shortly after the American Revolutionary War was won, Americans took to giving French names to cities and regions in tribute to their allies. In Kentucky alone, the names of Louisville, Versailles (where Woodford Reserve still stands), and Bourbon County attest to this gratitude. Admittedly, there are enduring links between whiskey production using corn (whereas early American whiskey had been dominated by rye) and Bourbon County, but, according to several historians, the name may have been thought up by the Tarascon brothers—two French traders who had moved to Louisville, and rode the tide of Francophilia and prerevolutionary nostalgia to attract the sizable French immigrant market in New Orleans.

In order to reduce evaporation, the earliest American whiskeys were often stored in earthenware jars, even though this hampered flavor development. The idea of aging whiskey in oak barrels was

la Whiskey Rebellion fait long feu. Les rebelles capitulent sans combattre lorsque Washington leur oppose une armée de 13 000 hommes : une guerre de sécession entre les États des côtes et la région de la vallée de l'Ohio vient d'être évitée.

ELIJAH CRAIG, ENTRÉ DANS LA LÉGENDE

Une ancienne tradition attribue à ce révérend l'invention du bourbon, mais tout porte aujourd'hui à croire que cette tradition remonte à des historiens du XIXᵉ siècle désireux d'attribuer à un homme d'Église la paternité d'un breuvage qui n'était pas toujours en odeur de sainteté.

D'OÙ VIENT LE NOM DE "BOURBON"?

Vaste mystère... Au lendemain de leur Guerre d'indépendance, les Américains baptisent de nombreuses villes et régions en hommage à leur allié français. Au Kentucky, les noms de Louisville, de Versailles (où se trouve encore Woodford Reserve) et du comté de Bourbon attestent de cette gratitude. Certes, il existe un lien entre la production de whiskey à base de maïs (alors que le seigle dominait dans la production des premiers whiskeys américains) et le comté de Bourbon, mais selon plusieurs historiens, cette appellation pourrait être née dans l'imagination des frères Tarascon, deux négociants français émigrés à Louisville, qui auraient su profiter de la francophilie ambiante et d'une certaine nostalgie prérévolutionnaire pour séduire l'important marché des émigrés français de La Nouvelle-Orléans.

Les premiers whiskeys américains sont souvent stockés dans des jarres de céramique, qui empêchent toute évaporation, mais n'apportent aucune saveur. L'idée de faire vieillir le whiskey dans des fûts de

taken up later. It was not until 1793 that the first advertisements were issued lauding barrel-aged whiskeys, and age was not mentioned on a whiskey bottle until 1814.

THE ERA OF BOTTLED WHISKY

Bourbon was first bottled in 1870, and the practice gathered pace with the passage of the Bottled in Bond Act of 1897 and the establishment of the earliest bottling plants in 1903. Bottling became the norm during Prohibition, when the sale of whiskey was permitted solely through pharmacies in the form of sealed, one-pint bottles.

The first bourbon to be sold exclusively in bottles was Old Forester, by George Garvin Brown, the founder of Brown-Forman. Initially, this was the Louisville-based trader's response to requests from the numerous physicians who regularly prescribed whiskey to relieve pain and other conditions. The law of 1897 also meant that, going forward, the contents of the bottle would be guaranteed by the Federal State.

Bottling constituted the only effective means of countering the practices of certain unscrupulous makers, who would "enrich" the contents of the barrels stored in whiskey bars with freshly distilled spirits, to which they would sometimes add lanolin to provide body or prune juice to alter its color and taste.

BREATHING IN THE BARREL

Though barrel-aging is one of the essential characteristics of all whisky, it takes on special importance in the case of bourbon. Variations in temperature are much greater in Kentucky and Tennessee than in Northern Europe.

chêne intervient plus tard. Il faudra attendre 1793 pour voir apparaître les premières publicités vantant des whiskeys vieillis, et 1814 pour que l'âge fasse son apparition sur certaines bouteilles.

L'ÈRE DU WHISKY EN BOUTEILLE

Les premières mises en bouteille de bourbon datent de 1870. Elles commencent à se généraliser avec le passage du Bottled in Bond Act en 1897 et de la création des premières usines de bouteilles en 1903. Elles deviennent la norme avec la Prohibition, quand la seule vente autorisée concerne les pharmacies, qui distribuent le whiskey dans des bouteilles scellées d'un volume d'une pinte.

Old Forester est le premier bourbon vendu exclusivement en bouteille par le fondateur de Brown-Forman, George Garvin Brown. Ce négociant basé à Louisville souhaitait à l'origine répondre à une demande formulée par de nombreux médecins, qui prescrivaient régulièrement du whiskey pour soulager certaines douleurs, par exemple. La loi de 1897 signifie que l'État fédéral est désormais garant du contenu des bouteilles.

La mise en bouteille constitue alors le seul moyen efficace de lutter contre les pratiques de certains fabricants peu scrupuleux qui n'hésitent pas à «enrichir» le contenu des fûts utilisés dans les auberges à l'aide d'eau-de-vie fraîchement distillée parfois enrichie de lanoline pour le corps et de jus de pruneau pour la couleur et le goût.

LA RESPIRATION DES FÛTS

Le vieillissement en fût est une caractéristique essentielle des whiskies, mais il revêt une importance particulière dans le cas du bourbon. En effet, les variations

As temperatures soar during the day, the pressure in the barrel increases, forcing a proportion of the contents into the wood, which is released only when the cool night falls. This daily cycle results in bourbon's particular flavor, since only new oak barrels are used. The barrels are first burned, or charred, to sterilize the wood, thereby creating a layer of filtering charcoal that aromatizes the contents and, in the case of new barrels, turns it a redder color. The United States's innovation essentially consisted in never using the barrels more than once, unlike the prevailing practices in Europe.

As a result, bourbon requires a briefer aging period than malt, since, after about twelve years, the woody taste can become overbearing. In the United States, as elsewhere, the age printed on the label is that of the youngest whiskey in the blend. In the absence of any such indication, its age is generally about four years (Maker's Mark and Jack Daniels being the most famous representatives in this category).

In the European tradition, on the other hand, traders reuse casks of Jerez (sherry—a Spanish white turned into a fortified wine), high-quality red Bordeaux (claret), port, or Madeira, enabling them to enrich the range of flavors of the whiskey with notes absorbed from alcoholic drinks long consumed and appreciated by the British, in contrast to the woody and vanilla flavors that usually result from the use of new barrels.

de température sont nettement plus importantes au Kentucky ou au Tennessee qu'elles ne le sont en Europe du Nord.

Chaque jour, lorsque la température s'élève, la pression dans le fût fait pénétrer une partie de son contenu dans le bois, dont il s'extrait plus tard, au retour des fraîcheurs nocturnes. C'est à ce cycle que le bourbon doit ses arômes si particuliers, puisqu'il utilise toujours des fûts de chêne neuf. Ces fûts font l'objet d'un brûlage, ou bousinage, qui stérilise le bois et crée une couche filtrante qui contribue à aromatiser leur contenu et, dans le cas des fûts neufs, à lui donner une coloration plus rouge. L'innovation des États-Unis a consisté, pour l'essentiel, à ne jamais réemployer les fûts, contrairement aux traditions en vigueur en Europe.

C'est aussi pour cette raison que le bourbon demande des durées de vieillissement moins importantes que les malts : la prédominance du bois peut devenir excessive après 12 ans. Aux États-Unis comme ailleurs, l'âge du whiskey le plus jeune de l'assemblage doit figurer sur l'étiquette. En l'absence d'indication, il s'agit la plupart du temps d'un 4 ans d'âge (Maker's Mark et Jack Daniels sont les représentants les plus célèbres de cette catégorie).

Dans la tradition Européenne, la réutilisation de fûts de xérès (ou « sherry », des vins blancs espagnols mutés à l'eau-de-vie), de grands vins rouges de Bordeaux («claret»), de porto ou de madère, permet aux marchands d'enrichir la palette aromatique de leur whiskies avec des notes issues de tous les alcools déjà consommés et appréciés de longue date par la population britannique (plutôt que les saveurs bois-vanille habituellement conférées par les fûts neufs).

III |
Conquering
the World

The history of whisky has been forged against the backdrop of great catastrophes of the nineteenth and twentieth centuries—from the phylloxera epidemic that devastated European vineyards in the second half of the nineteenth century to the global conflicts of the twentieth, not forgetting other historic events, such as Prohibition in the United States.

In early nineteenth-century France, at a time when America was all the rage, a number of winegrowers fell for a black grape called Isabella, a variety from Pennsylvania whose berries had a hint of raspberry and that seemed particularly resistant to parasites. Unfortunately, the imported stocks were infested with an aphid that was soon decimating the local vines: phylloxera.

Deprived of their claret (red wine imported from Bordeaux) and brandy (cognac, in particular), British high society discovered a fondness for Scottish whisky. Distilleries increased in number to such an extent that, by the end of the century, Irish and Scottish whiskies were suffering from overproduction.

The crisis worsened with the onset of World War I, when producers were ordered to produce alcohol almost exclusively for medicinal or military use. The war had another, less direct effect: the imposition of a two-year warehousing bond period—a practice already in force in Ireland—that was later raised to three years, has resulted in what today constitutes one of the salient characteristics of whisky.

III |
À la conquête
du monde

Le destin du whisky se forge à l'aune des grandes catastrophes historiques du xixe et du xxe siècle, depuis l'épidémie de phylloxéra qui ravage l'Europe pendant la seconde moitié du xixe siècle aux grandes guerres du xxe, sans oublier, bien sûr, d'autres grands événements comme l'épisode de la Prohibition aux États-Unis.

En France, au début du xixe siècle, l'Amérique est à la mode, et certains viticulteurs s'enthousiasment pour l'Isabelle à grains noirs, une vigne originaire de Pennsylvanie dont les raisins ont des arômes de framboise et qui se montre particulièrement résistante aux parasites. Malheureusement, les ceps importés sont infestés d'un puceron qui ne tardera pas à décimer les récoltes viticoles françaises : le phylloxéra.

Privée de « claret » (c'est-à-dire de vin rouge importé de Bordeaux) et de brandy (en particulier de cognac), la haute société britannique se découvre un nouvel appétit pour le whisky importé d'Écosse. Les distilleries se multiplient au point de provoquer une surproduction de whiskies irlandais et écossais à la fin du siècle.

La crise s'aggrave avec l'arrivée de la Première Guerre mondiale. Tous les producteurs sont sommés de produire presque exclusivement de l'alcool à usage médical ou militaire. Cette guerre aura une autre conséquence indirecte : l'imposition d'une période de garde sous entrepôt de deux ans, pratique déjà en vigueur chez les Irlandais, et qui, en passant à trois ans, deviendra l'une des caractéristiques essentielles du whisky.

THE END OF IRISH SUPREMACY

In the 1780s, Ireland possessed vast distilleries, and its four largest producers—John Power, John Jameson, William Jameson, and George Roe—dominated the international market, with the United States as the main outlet. By the early twentieth century, Ireland was exporting 400 different brands to America.

From the end of the nineteenth century, however, Irish hegemony was slipping. Scotland was catching up, and, thanks to the installation of Coffey stills, it soon multiplied the output of Lowlands distilleries by a factor of ten. These stills, whose yield is far higher than that of classic pot stills, never made inroads into Ireland, despite being invented by one

IRLANDE : FIN D'UNE DOMINATION

Dès les années 1780, l'Irlande dispose d'immenses distilleries et ses quatre grands producteurs, John Power, John Jameson, William Jameson et George Roe, dominent le marché international, avec les États-Unis pour principale débouchée. L'Irlande y exportera jusqu'à 400 marques différentes au début du XXe siècle.

Mais cette domination irlandaise commence à diminuer dès la fin du XIXe siècle. L'Écosse rattrape alors une partie de son retard en décuplant la capacité de production de ses distilleries des Lowlands grâce à l'installation d'alambics Coffey. Ces alambics, au rendement bien plus important que les pot stills traditionnels, sont boudés par l'Irlande, bien qu'ils aient

of its countrymen. The point of no return was to be reached during Prohibition, when the Irish, beset by moral scruples, left the immense American bootleg market to the Scots. Moreover, Eire's accession to independence in 1922 led to a trade war that cut the country off from the English market. It took until the 1980s for Irish whiskey to fully recover: it is now flourishing.

By the early twentieth century, the issue of establishing on official definition for whisky had been addressed on both sides of the Atlantic. In Great Britain, a British royal commission in 1909 stipulated an administrative definition of whisky's composition that covered, together with malts, spirits made from other grains, as well as blends. That same year, US President William Howard Taft personally brought down the curtain on a debate over the purity of American whiskey that had lasted three years by decreeing the existence of two categories: "straight" and "blended."

Consolidated by these clarifications and aware of the undeniable importance of whiskey to the American economy (its duties generated some of the highest tax revenues prior to the imposition of income tax in 1913), distillers tended not to take the advocates of prohibition seriously enough, failing to organize themselves in time to prevent the passing of the Volstead Act on January 16, 1920. And thus, for thirteen years, all sales of whiskey were prohibited throughout the US.

Paradoxically, Prohibition would convert many a beer and bourbon drinker to the virtues of scotch. In order to satisfy the demand for hard liquor, numerous bootleggers were not above concocting moonshine from industrial ethanol, caramel, and water that they would pass off as bourbon.

été inventés par l'un de ses ressortissants. Le point de non-retour sera atteint pendant la Prohibition, quand les Irlandais, par scrupule moral, abandonnent l'immense marché des bootleggers américains aux Écossais. En parallèle, leur accession à l'Indépendance, en 1922, aboutit à une guerre commerciale qui les coupe du marché anglais. Il faudra attendre la fin les années 1980 pour assister à une renaissance du whisky irlandais, désormais florissant.

Au début du xxᵉ siècle, la question de l'identité officielle du whisky se pose des deux côtés de l'Atlantique. En Grande-Bretagne, une commission royale britannique définit en 1909 la composition officielle du whisky, et inclut, au côté des malts, les eaux-de-vie d'autres céréales et les blends. La même année, le président américain William Howard Taft met personnellement fin à trois ans de débats sur la pureté du whiskey américain et décrète l'existence de deux catégories: «straight» et «blended».

Forts de cette clarification et du rôle crucial du whiskey dans l'économie américaine (ses taxes génèrent certains des revenus fiscaux les plus importants avant la création de l'impôt sur le revenu, en 1913), les distillateurs ne prennent pas les partisans de la prohibition au sérieux et ne s'organisent pas à temps pour prévenir le passage du Volstead Act, le 16 janvier 1920. Pendant 13 ans, toute vente de whiskey sera interdite sur le territoire américain.

Paradoxalement, la Prohibition aura pour effet de convertir de nombreux buveurs de bière et de bourbon en amateurs de scotch whisky. En effet, pour répondre à la demande de spiritueux, certains bootleggers n'hésitent pas à bricoler des concoctions à base d'éthanol industriel, de caramel et d'eau, et à les faire passer pour du bourbon. Face à ces ersatz qui

In response to these blatant counterfeit liquors, the Scots developed products tailor-made for the American market. This was the case with Cutty Sark, for instance, created on March 23, 1923, which met with great success. These initiatives made a crucial difference: while bourbon producers were being ruined, the reputation of Scottish makers was on the rise, and the Scottish origin of a bottle gradually became a mark of quality throughout the US market.

FOR MEDICINAL USE, ONLY

One of the means adopted to circumvent Prohibition consisted of emphasizing the medicinal virtues of whiskey and selling it through pharmacists. (Similarly, wine, while less common in North America, remained available because of its use in the Christian liturgy.) During the thirteen years that Prohibition lasted, six distilleries were authorized to produce whiskey for sale in pharmacies and on prescription: Brown-Forman, Glenmore, Frankfort Distilleries (later Four Roses), Schenley, American Medicinal Spirits (or AMS, the only one that did not manufacture its own whiskey), and the distillery A. P. Stitzel (subsequently to become Stitzel-Weller). Bottles dating from Prohibition are less rare than one might imagine, but their value is essentially historical, because the whiskey they contain is rather homogenous and uninteresting in terms of taste.

A QUEST FOR EXCELLENCE FROM THE LAND OF THE RISING SUN

The history of whisky in Japan began with a diplomatic mission dispatched to the country by US President Millard Fillmore in 1853. In his memoirs,

ne dupent personne, les Écossais réagissent et développent des produits adaptés au marché américain. C'est le cas de Cutty Sark, par exemple, créé le 23 mars 1923, qui rencontre un grand succès. De telles initiatives sont déterminantes : tandis que les producteurs de bourbon sont décimés, la réputation des marques écossaises ne cesse de croître, et l'origine écossaise d'une bouteille s'impose progressivement comme un gage de qualité à travers tout le marché américain.

VOIE ORALE UNIQUEMENT

L'un des moyens adoptés pour contourner la Prohibition consistait à s'appuyer sur les vertus médicales du whiskey et à le vendre en pharmacie (tandis que le vin, moins présent outre-Atlantique, restait proposé en vertu de son utilité religieuse...). Pendant les 13 ans que durera la Prohibition, six distilleries sont autorisées à produire du whiskey destiné à la vente en pharmacie et sur ordonnance : Brown-Forman, Glenmore, Frankfort Distilleries (qui deviendra Four Roses), Schenley, American Medicinal Spirits (ou AMS, la seule qui ne fabriquait pas son propre whiskey) et la distillerie A. Ph. Stitzel (qui deviendra Stitzel-Weller). Les bouteilles datant de la Prohibition sont moins rares qu'on ne l'imagine, mais leur valeur est avant tout historique, car elles contiennent un whiskey très standardisé sans grand intérêt gustatif.

UNE VOLONTÉ D'EXCELLENCE AU PAYS DU SOLEIL LEVANT

L'histoire du whisky au Japon commence avec une mission diplomatique diligentée par le président américain Millard Fillmore en 1853. Dans ses mémoires, le Commodore Matthew Calbraith Perry précise que le whiskey a joué un rôle essentiel dans le succès de sa

HOKKAIDO

Yoichi • Sapporo

SEA OF JAPAN

Noshiro

Miyagikyo Sendai

Hanyu*

JAPAN

Chichibu

Agano

Karuizawa

Shinano

Hakushu

Shinshu• Tokyo

Monde

Kyoto

Gotemba

Yamazaki

Osaka

White Hoak

PACIFIC OCEAN

* Distilleries
not currently in use /
Distilleries en sommeil

Commodore Matthew Calbraith Perry outlined how whiskey fulfilled a key role in the success of this delegation, playing its part in overcoming the reticence of the Japanese, who had long been hostile to forging any viable commercial links with the West.

The Scots, however, benefited the most from this burgeoning market. In 1873, the Iwakura mission returned from Europe with a case of Old Parr, an event that seems to have sparked the national predilection for Scottish blends.

In 1918, Masataka Taketsuru, a Hiroshima native, traveled to Scotland to take lessons in organic chemistry and to master the art of making whisky. After a stint at the University of Glasgow and having met Jessie Roberta Cowan, the woman who was later to become

mission, en contribuant à désarmer les réticences des Japonais, très longtemps hostiles à toute véritable ouverture commerciale avec l'Occident.

Pourtant, ce seront les Écossais qui profiteront le plus de cette ouverture. En 1873, la délégation d'Iwakura revient d'une mission en Europe avec une caisse d'Old Parr, qui semble avoir déclenché une prédilection nationale pour les blends écossais.

En 1918, Masataka Taketsuru, un natif d'Hiroshima, arrive en Écosse pour y suivre des cours de chimie organique et s'initier à la fabrication du whisky. Après un passage à l'université de Glasgow et la rencontre de celle qui deviendra son épouse, il est apprenti dans les distilleries de Longmorn, puis Hazelburn. À son retour, deux ans plus tard, Shin-

his wife, he served an apprenticeship at the distilleries of Longmorn and then Hazelburn. On his return home two years later, he was invited by Shinjiro Torii—a one-time wine merchant who had decided to branch out into the manufacture of whisky with Suntory (then known as Kotobukiya)—to build and manage a distillery at Yamazaki, near Kyoto. His first creation, christened Shiro Fuda, proved too smoky for the Japanese public's palate. In 1934, Taketsuru left Suntory to found his own distillery, Yoichi, on Hokkaido, which was to become the first of the Nikka brand. For his part, Shinjiro Torii concentrated his efforts on identifying and catering to Japanese tastes. Finally, in 1937, he created Kakubin, which remains the best-selling brand in Japan.

THE GODMOTHER OF JAPANESE WHISKY

It all began at Kirkintilloch in 1918 with the meeting between Jessie Roberta Cowan (later known as Rita Taketsuru) and Masataka Taketsuru—a chemistry student at the University of Glasgow who had come to Scotland to learn about whisky making. They wed in 1920, and together left Scotland for Japan a few years later.

Rita played an essential role in Nikka's early years. In the isolated environment of Hokkaido Island, she managed to integrate herself completely into the local culture at a time when mixed marriages were extremely rare. For a long time she was the bread-winner, teaching English and piano, and she also introduced her husband to a number of investors who helped him establish a business of his own.

Wartime was particularly difficult for Rita. Many Japanese, even her own adopted daughter, held her background against her, and the authorities even suspected the couple of espionage because of a radio

jiro Torii, un ancien négociant en vins qui a décidé de se lancer dans la fabrication de whisky avec Suntory, qui s'appelle alors Kotobukiya, l'invite à construire et à prendre la direction d'une distillerie située à Yamazaki, près de Kyoto. Sa première réalisation est baptisée Shiro Fuda, mais se révèle trop fumée pour le public japonais.

En 1934, Taketsuru quitte Suntory pour fonder sa propre distillerie, Yoichi, sur Hokkaïdo, qui sera la première de la marque Nikka. De son côté, Shinjiro Torii s'efforce d'identifier et de répondre aux préférences japonaises. Il crée enfin, en 1937, Kakubin qui reste la marque la plus vendue au Japon.

LA MARRAINE DU WHISKY JAPONAIS

Tout commence par une rencontre à Kirkintilloch, en 1918, entre Jessie Roberta « Rita » Cowan et Masataka Taketsuru, un étudiant en chimie de l'université de Glasgow venu en Écosse pour s'initier à la fabrication du whisky. Ils se marient en 1920, puis quittent ensemble l'Écosse, quelques années plus tard, pour le Japon.

Rita jouera un rôle essentiel dans les premières années de Nikka. Dans l'environnement isolé de l'île d'Hokkaïdo, elle parvient à s'intégrer totalement à la culture locale à une période où les mariages mixtes sont rarissimes. Enseignant l'anglais et le piano, elle subvient longtemps aux besoins du foyer et présente à son époux des investisseurs susceptibles de l'aider à faire décoller son entreprise.

La Deuxième Guerre mondiale est pour elle une épreuve douloureuse. De nombreux Japonais, y compris sa propre fille adoptive, lui reprochent ses origines, et les autorités soupçonnent même le couple d'espionnage en raison de l'antenne radio dont leur

antenna on their house. But they held firm and, in a country deprived of imports during the years of conflict, Masataka Taketsuru's whisky soon proved a success. Rita Taketsuru, who passed away in 1961 at the age of sixty-three, remains a legendary figure in Japan; there was even a TV series inspired by her life, entitled "Massan", broadcast in 2014.

BLENDS AND SINGLE MALTS

From 1850 to 1960, Scotch whisky conquered the world thanks to its blends, in which malt whisky is mixed with grain whisky. Aging is generally the work of traders rather than distillers. The first great blend dates from 1853: "Usher's OVG" (Old Vatted Glenlivet), a blend of several whiskies from the area of Glenlivet.

Until the beginning of the 1970s, whiskies from only one distillery and made from 100% malted barley were known as "Pure Malt." The United Kingdom subsequently entered a period of recession, and a number of distilleries were mothballed by their proprietors. Because the minimum aging duration is three years, many casks therefore became "orphaned." Some traders decided to buy up these whiskies, designating those from a single distillery as "single malts."

The principle behind blending is far older and results from the opening of the market brought about by the ratification of the Excise Act in 1823. At that time, it became imperative to be able to offer consistent quality in conjunction with significant output. The inspiration came from a practice that was widespread in France, where for many years older and younger cognacs had been mixed to obtain a uniform product better adapted to retailing in large quantities. In modern parlance, "marrying"— in which casks from the same distillery are mixed,

maison est dotée. Mais ils tiennent bon et le whisky de Masataka Taketsuru ne tarde pas à rencontrer le succès, dans un pays privé de toute importation par ces années de conflit. Disparue en 1961, à l'âge de 63 ans, Rita Taketsuru reste une figure légendaire au Japon, ayant même eu les honneurs d'une série télévisée inspirée de sa vie, *Massan*, diffusée en 2014.

BLENDS ET SINGLE MALTS

De 1850 à 1960, le whisky écossais conquiert le monde grâce à ses blends, qui associent whisky de malt et whisky de grain. Le vieillissement est généralement pris en charge par les marchands et non par les distillateurs eux-mêmes. Le premier grand blend date de 1853. C'est « Usher's OVG », qui signifie Old Vatted Glenlivet et assemble plusieurs whiskies de la région de Glenlivet.

Jusqu'au début des années 1970, les whiskies provenant d'une seule distillerie, élaborés à partir de 100 % d'orge maltée, sont connus sous l'appellation « Pure Malt ». Par la suite, le Royaume-Uni entre dans une période de récession, et un certain nombre de distilleries sont mises en sommeil par leurs propriétaires. La durée minimum de vieillissement étant de trois ans, de nombreux fûts se retrouvèrent « orphelins ». Des négociants eurent alors l'idée de les racheter en distinguant les whiskies provenant d'une même distillerie comme des « single malt ».

Le principe de l'assemblage est plus ancien, et résulte de l'ouverture du marché déclenchée par la promulgation de l'Excise Act en 1823. Il devient alors indispensable de proposer une qualité constante à des volumes importants. On s'inspire de la pratique répandue en France, où l'on assemble depuis des années les cognacs anciens et jeunes pour obtenir un produit normalisé, adapté à une commercialisation à grande échelle.

giving rise to a single malt—is thus distinguished from "blending"—the combination of malt whiskies and grain whiskies from various distilleries.

POSTWAR TRIUMPHS

Although many distilleries had been forced to close in the wake of new restrictions imposed during World War II, whisky remained a valuable exchange currency that, for Great Britain, facilitated the payment of essential goods. By the time the conflict finally came to an end, though, stocks in Scotland, Ireland, and the United States were totally exhausted. Resuming production was a priority for the British government, which focused on exports to the US and Canada.

By the end of the 1950s, production was soaring. From the 1960s, the lion's share of distilleries replaced their malting floors with mechanical plants, while oil burners ousted coal-burning kilns and indirect steam heating became the norm. Sherry butts were still few and far between, and many European producers were forced to import American oak barrels that modified the character of the product.

In Japan, meanwhile, Masataka Taketsuru built his company's second distillery, Miyagikyo, on the island of Honshu in 1969. As for Shinjiro Torii, he launched a chain of bars, Tory's, that was instrumental in popularizing his successive blends (Tory's Whisky, Suntory Old, Suntory Royal), as well as his very first single malt, Yamazaki Single Malt, in 1984.

The world of whisky has been continually affected by crises and reorganization, with the growing influence of large groups, such as Pernod-Ricard, Seagram, and Grand Metropolitan and Guinness PLC, whose merger in 1997 was to create Diageo.

Dans la terminologie contemporaine, on distingue le *marrying* (mariage) qui en mélangeant les fûts d'une même distillerie, donne naissance à un single malt, du *blend* (assemblage), qui associe whisky de malt et whisky de grain de différentes distilleries.

L'ESSOR DE L'APRÈS-GUERRE

De nouvelles restrictions s'imposent pendant la Seconde Guerre mondiale, et de nombreuses distilleries doivent fermer. Mais le whisky est une monnaie d'échange précieuse et permet à la Grande-Bretagne, par exemple, de se procurer des biens de première nécessité. Quand le conflit prend fin, les stocks sont épuisés en Écosse, en Irlande et aux États-Unis. La reprise de la production est une priorité pour le gouvernement britannique, qui privilégie l'exportation vers les États-Unis et le Canada.

La fin des années 1950 correspond à une très forte production. Les aires de maltage sont remplacées par le maltage mécanique pour un grand nombre de distilleries à partir des années 1960, les fours à charbon sont remplacés par des brûleurs à fuel, le chauffage indirect à vapeur devient la norme. Les fûts de sherry se font rares et de nombreux producteurs européens sont contraints d'importer des fûts de chêne américains, ce qui modifie le caractère de leur production.

Au Japon, Masataka Taketsuru bâtit la seconde distillerie de sa société, Miyagikyo, sur l'île de Honshū, en 1969. Shinjiro Torii, lui, lance une chaîne de bars, Tory's, qui contribue à populariser ses blends successifs (Tory's Whisky, Suntory Old, Suntory Royal...), puis son tout premier single malt, en 1984, Yamazaki Single Malt.

Les crises et les restructurations se succèdent dans le monde du whisky, avec une présence croissante de

The sector has also been rocked by historical events, such as the Vietnam War and the 1970s oil crisis, as well as the recession of the early 1980s, during which a significant number of distilleries had to shut down. As the twentieth century progressed, each type of whisky gradually honed its identity, not only in terms of flavor, but also in respect of its brand image. Today, there is a revival of interest in malts and bourbons in every variation. The traditional, old-fashioned connotations long associated with such spirits have practically faded away, and the customer base continues to widen. Customers are increasingly exacting, but they are also more curious and open to innovation. With distilleries springing up all over the world, the discoveries that await enthusiasts seem limitless.

grands groupes comme Pernod-Ricard, Seagram ou encore Grand Metropolitan et Guinness PLC, dont la fusion créera Diageo en 1997. Le secteur est également touché par les événements historiques comme la guerre du Vietnam et la crise pétrolière des années 1970, ainsi que la récession du début des années 1980, qui entraîne la fermeture d'un grand nombre de distilleries.

Au fil du xxe siècle, chaque type de whisky affine progressivement son identité, tant sur le plan des arômes que sur celui de son image de marque. On observe aujourd'hui un regain de passion pour les malts et les bourbons dans toutes leurs déclinaisons. Les connotations traditionnelles vieillissantes qui lui sont longtemps restées associées ont presque totalement disparu et les amateurs se diversifient. Leurs palais se font plus exigeants, mais aussi plus curieux et ouverts à la nouveauté. De nombreuses distilleries se créent à travers le monde et l'univers de découverte qui s'offre aux passionnés ne cesse de repousser ses limites.

IV |
New Whisky Producers

At one time limited to Scotland, the world of single malt and of whisky in general is increasingly open to new producers and new techniques. Today, one comes across single malts from San Francisco and from the foothills of the Himalayas, while countries such as France, Italy, Germany, Wales, New Zealand, and Australia have also entered the fray. There are plenty of treasures to be unearthed, and whisky lovers can enjoy the frequently remarkable character of these new offerings.

It would be pointless, however, to try to list every country now producing whisky. Moreover, developments in this area are never-ending. By way of review, we will instead deal with three exemplary cases, three new arrivals in the galaxy of single malts, together with their leading brands. These countries—India, Sweden, and Taiwan—have all been adroit enough to impose unique styles that nevertheless retain the essential principles that underpin the art of whisky making.

INDIA: FROM FICTION TO REALITY

India is the world's number one whisky consumer. This record, however, may be somewhat misleading, since India is the only country where blends are permitted to include neutral spirits distilled from molasses, a practice culturally and historically explained by the fact that the country has long remained prey to poor harvests. In addition, sky-high import duties have tended to keep scotch and

IV |
Les nouveaux acteurs

Jadis limité à l'Écosse, le monde du single malt, et du whisky en général, ne cesse de s'ouvrir à de nouveaux acteurs et à de nouvelles pratiques. On trouve désormais des single malt provenant aussi bien de San Francisco que des contreforts de l'Himalaya. Des pays comme la France, l'Italie, l'Allemagne, le Pays de Galle, la Nouvelle-Zélande et l'Australie ne sont pas en reste. On y trouve parfois de vraies pépites, et les amateurs ne peuvent que se réjouir du caractère souvent inattendu de toutes ces nouvelles propositions.

Il serait vain d'évoquer ici tous ces nouveaux pays du whisky, qui, du reste, sont en constante évolution. En guise de tour d'horizon, analysons trois cas exemplaires, trois jeunes acteurs du single malt et leurs marques phare, qui toutes ont eu l'intelligence d'imposer des styles uniques tout en conservant l'essentiel des principes qui caractérisent l'art du whisky: l'Inde, la Suède et Taïwan.

L'INDE : DU MOT À LA CHOSE

L'Inde affiche la plus grande consommation mondiale de whisky, mais ce record est purement nominatif, puisqu'il s'agit du seul pays où les blends peuvent inclure de l'alcool neutre distillé à partir de mélasse. Cela s'explique historiquement et culturellement par le fait que le pays est resté longtemps sujet aux mauvaises récoltes. D'autre part, des droits de douane prohibitifs ont mis les scotchs et autres bourbons

bourbon out of the reach of the general public. As a result, whisky of Scottish origin is one of the most prestigious traditional presents to give on Dewali, the most important Hindu festival.

The arrival of malt whisky in India dates back to the late 1820s, during the British colonial era, when George Dyer built the country's first distillery at Kasauli, in the shadow of the Himalayas. The distillery remains active today.

Today, the big name in Indian whisky is Amrut. The distillery has been in existence since 1948, but in 1982 Neelakanta Rao Jagdale decided to produce a whisky hat contained both malted and unmalted barley. After working on the first batch for eighteen months, it was not bottled straight from the cask but mixed with molasses alcohol to produce MaQintosh Premium Whisky.

It took time for the brand to make inroads abroad. As you can imagine, the angels' share is particularly high in India (11–12% instead of the 2–4% in Scotland), but, on the plus side, some whiskies aged for only four to five years present profiles that stand comparison with much older single malt scotches. In 2003, a specialized public house in Glasgow, the Pot Still, staged a blind tasting at which it made a strong impression on the connoisseurs gathered there, including specialist John Lamond, who compared it to Japanese single malts.

While respecting the traditions of single malt, the distillery is gradually shifting its emphasis to expressions with more original aromatic profiles no longer limited to imitating Scottish models. Thus Amrut Fusion, aged for little more than three years, combines unpeated barley from India with Scottish peaty malt. Its consecration occurred in the 2010 edition of *Jim Murray's Whisky Bible*, in which the author awarded third place

hors de portée du grand public. Ceci étant, le scotch d'origine écossaise fait partie des cadeaux traditionnels les plus prestigieux offerts à l'occasion de Divali, la fête la plus importante de la religion hindoue.

L'arrivée du whisky de malt en Inde date de la fin des années 1820, à l'époque de la colonisation britannique, avec la construction de la première distillerie du pays à Kasauli, en lisière de l'Himalaya, par George Dyer. Cette distillerie est toujours en activité de nos jours.

Aujourd'hui, le grand nom du whisky en Inde est Amrut. La distillerie existe depuis 1948, mais en 1982, Neelakanta Rao Jagdale décide d'y produire un whisky à partir d'orge maltée et non maltée. Son premier batch, après 18 mois de travail, n'est pas mis en bouteille tel quel, mais associé à de l'alcool de mélasse pour produire le MaQintosh Premium Whisky.

La marque hésite longtemps à se lancer à l'étranger. Comme on peut l'imaginer, la part des anges est particulièrement élevée en Inde (de 11 à 12 % au lieu de 2 à 4 % en Écosse), mais en contrepartie certains whiskies vieillis uniquement 4 à 5 ans présentent des profils comparables aux single malt écossais bien plus âgés. Ainsi, dès 2003, un pub spécialisé de Glasgow, le Pot Still, proposa un test à l'aveugle qui fit forte impression aux amateurs éclairés réunis, dont le spécialiste John Lamond, qui le compara aux single malt japonais.

Tout en respectant la tradition du single malt, la distillerie s'oriente progressivement vers des expressions aux profils aromatiques originaux, qui ne se cantonnent plus à imiter les modèles écossais. Ainsi, Amrut Fusion associe une orge non tourbée provenant d'Inde à un malt tourbé d'Écosse, et vieilli pendant un peu plus de trois ans. La consécration arrive dans l'édition 2010 de la *Whisky Bible*, où Jim Murray attribue la

to Armut Fusion Single Malt in his international classification of the best single malts.

TAIWAN:
SUCCESS IN A TROPICAL CLIMATE

Taiwan is another country with an insatiable appetite for single malt, so much so that today it represents the fourth most valuable market for whisky on the planet. The local climate was long regarded as unsuitable for whisky production, but for the last few years the island has been home to an important player in the world of top-flight whisky: Kavalan.

Kavalan—which means "plainsmen"—is the name of an ancient aboriginal people who occupied the northeast of the island of Taiwan prior to the arrival of the Chinese at the end of the eighteenth century. Located an hour from Taipei, at Yi-Lan, the young distillery of Kavalan receives nearly a million visitors a year—as many as all the distilleries of Scotland combined. Founded by the King Car group, it focuses its efforts on top-of-the-line product. With this goal in mind, it has imported two pairs of Forsyth stills from Scotland and brought in international experts, including Jim Swan, who supervised a first new-make issued on March 11, 2006. A little more than two years later, the distillery brought out its debut whisky.

A blind tasting organized by *The Times* of London in 2010 provided experts with the opportunity to compare bottles of Kavalan with various Scottish single malts of the same age. The panel was surprised to find that they had unquestionably granted first place to the Taiwanese newcomer. Today, the reputation of Kavalan is based particularly on its exceptional single casks, which have carried off many awards.

3ᵉ place à Armut Fusion Single Malt dans son classement international des meilleurs single malts.

TAÏWAN :
UNE RÉUSSITE SOUS CLIMAT TROPICAL

Taïwan fait partie de ces pays où le single malt est très apprécié, au point qu'il s'agit aujourd'hui du quatrième marché du whisky mondial en valeur. Le climat local a longtemps été considéré comme inadapté à la production de whisky, mais depuis quelques années, l'île héberge un acteur de taille dans le monde des whiskies d'exception : Kavalan.

Le nom Kavalan (qui signifie «hommes des plaines») est celui d'une ancienne tribu aborigène qui occupait le nord-est de l'île de Taïwan avant l'arrivée des Chinois, à la fin du XVIIIᵉ siècle. Située à Yi-Lan, à une heure de Taipei, la jeune distillerie taïwanaise de Kavalan accueille près d'un million de visiteurs par an, soit autant que toutes les distilleries d'Écosse réunies. Fondée par le groupe King Car, la distillerie a axé ses efforts sur une production haut de gamme. Pour cela, elle a importé deux paires d'alambics Forsyth d'Écosse et fait appel à des experts internationaux tels que Jim Swan, qui a supervisé la création de son premier new-make, paru le 11 mars 2006. Un peu plus de deux ans plus tard, la distillerie commercialisait son tout premier whisky.

Un test à l'aveugle organisé par le *Times* de Londres en 2010 a permis à un panel d'experts de comparer des bouteilles de Kavalan à divers single malt écossais du même âge. Ces experts, non sans surprise, ont alors accordé une première place incontestée à ce nouveau venu taïwanais. Aujourd'hui, la réputation de Kavalan tient en particulier à des single casks exceptionnels qui ont remporté de nombreux prix.

In 2016, the distillery was named Whisky Producer of the Year at the IWSC competition.

SWEDEN: ZEAL REWARDED

If Sweden's traditional spirit is aquavit—a grain alcohol that is not aged—Scandinavia as a whole contains the strongest concentration of clubs devoted to single malt in the world, while Stockholm hosts Taste Experience, the biggest beer and whisky festival on the planet.

The country's flagship distillery is Mackmyra, founded in 1999 by a group of student enthusiasts in a craft village 125 miles (200 km) from Stockholm. Now quoted on the stock exchange, Mackmyra long survived thanks to private individuals who put their names down for its eight-US-gallon (30-liter) casks. Today, it stands at the heart of a village dedicated to whisky-themed events, which attracts visitors in droves.

The distillery's water is supplied by an underground spring fed by the mountains of Valboåsen. Casks are stored in a disused mine in Bodås, which is also the site of the distillery's blending laboratory. Since the distillery's inception, its founders' ambition has been to obtain expressions that reflect typically Swedish aromatic profiles. To that aim, the casks are built from oaks cut down on a nearby island, and the distillery uses a local barley, which is heated by a fire fed by peat and juniper wood. Finally, certain finishings take place in casks that previously contained cloudberry (a kind of local blackberry) cordial, or even *glögg*, the Swedish mulled wine.

These bold innovations have been a great success: in 2016, Mackmyra won seven medals (including five gold) at the Wizard of Whisky World Awards.

La distillerie a été nommée Whisky Producer of the Year au concours IWSC 2016.

LA SUÈDE: LA PASSION RÉCOMPENSÉE

L'eau-de-vie traditionnelle de Suède est l'aquavit, un alcool de grain non vieillissant, mais la Scandinavie, dans son ensemble, affiche la plus forte concentration au monde de clubs consacrés au single malt, et Stockholm accueille le plus grand festival mondial de la bière et du whisky, Taste Experience.

La distillerie phare du pays est Mackmyra. Elle a été fondée en 1999 par un groupe d'étudiants enthousiastes, dans un village d'artisans situé à 200 km de Stockholm. Aujourd'hui cotée en bourse, Mackmyra a longtemps survécu grâce à des particuliers qui acceptaient d'acheter des fûts de 30 litres. Aujourd'hui, elle est au cœur d'un véritable village d'animations autour du whisky qui accueille un grand nombre de visiteurs.

La distillerie s'approvisionne en eau dans une source souterraine alimentée par les monts Valboåsen. Ses fûts sont entreposés dans une mine désaffectée à Bodås, où se trouve également le laboratoire d'assemblage de la distillerie. L'ambition des fondateurs, depuis l'origine, a été d'obtenir des expressions reflétant des profils aromatiques typiquement suédois. Pour cela, leurs fûts sont notamment réalisés à partir de chênes provenant d'une île voisine. La distillerie recourt également à une orge locale, chauffée par un feu de tourbe et de bois de genévrier. Enfin, certains affinages utilisent des fûts ayant contenu du vin de plaquebière (une sorte de mûre locale) ou même du *glögg*, équivalent suédois du vin chaud. Ces audaces sont couronnées de succès, puisque Mackmyra a remporté sept médailles (dont cinq d'or) aux Wizard of Whisky Awards 2016.

THE MICRO-DISTILLERY PHENOMENON

Since the dawn of the millennium, micro-distilleries have been mushrooming all over the world. This trend, coming hard on the heels of a renewed interest in microbreweries, has primarily concerned the United States, although its effects have also been felt in Italy, France, Japan, and Australia, notably Tasmania.

Generally the initiative of individuals or small companies, these whisky-making ventures take place on a small or medium scale in farms, garages, or warehouses. The expression "craft distillery" generally designates micro-distilleries that take their inspiration from the pioneering family tradition of North America. It suggests (although it does not guarantee) greater personal investment in manufacture, and the use of traditional materials and methods, with the accent on authentic raw materials.

The trend has even had an impact on a number of larger firms, which have not hesitated to set up micro-distilleries within their structures and produce batches quite different from the rest of their production, such as Beam Suntory at Maker's Mark and the Sazerac group at Buffalo Trace. The Heaven Hill distillery has opened a brand-new micro-distillery at the core of the Evan Williams Bourbon Experiment, one of Louisville's great attractions.

The human scale of these distilleries affords them a certain flexibility, allowing them to carry out bold experiments with the ingredients used, as well as with production methods and aging. Such enterprise enables them to create unique and original batches in small quantities, which, having tickled the fancy of drinkers in cocktail bars all over the United States, are today winning the hearts of customers from other parts of the world, too.

LE PHÉNOMÈNE DES MICRO-DISTILLERIES

Les micro-distilleries se multiplient à travers le monde depuis le début des années 2000. Cette vogue, issue d'un regain d'intérêt pour les micro-brasseries, touche avant tout les États-Unis, mais aussi l'Italie, la France, le Japon ou la Tasmanie, pour n'en citer que quelques-uns.

Il s'agit généralement d'initiatives d'individus ou de petites sociétés qui se lancent dans l'aventure d'une fabrication à petite ou moyenne échelle depuis leurs fermes, garages ou autres entrepôts. L'expression « craft distillery » désigne, d'une façon générale, les micro-distilleries s'inspirant de la tradition des familles pionnières nord-américaines. Elle suggère (mais ne garantit pas !) une implication personnelle plus importante dans la fabrication et un recours à des matériaux et à des méthodes traditionnels, avec un accent sur l'authenticité de la matière première.

Cette tendance touche même certains grands groupes, qui n'hésitent pas à installer des micro-distilleries au sein de leurs structures et à produire des batchs sans rapport avec le reste de leur production, comme Beam Suntory à Maker's Mark et le groupe Sazerac à Buffalo Trace. La distillerie Heaven Hill possède également une micro-distillerie rutilante au cœur de l'Evan Williams Bourbon Experience, l'une des attractions de Louisville.

La taille humaine de ces distilleries leur donne la souplesse nécessaire pour oser toute sorte d'expériences, tant sur les ingrédients utilisés que sur les méthodes de production ou de vieillissement. Une audace qui leur permet de créer en petite quantité des batchs uniques et originaux, qui après avoir su séduire la clientèle des bars à cocktails aux États-Unis, gagnent aujourd'hui le cœur de nombreux amateurs à travers le monde.

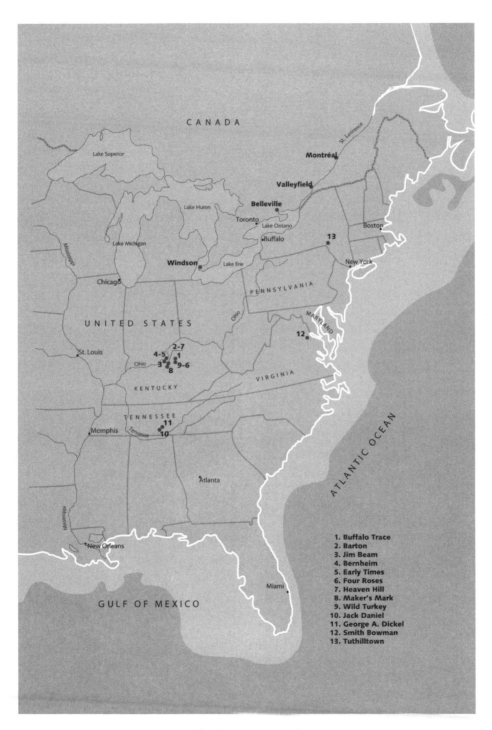

1. Buffalo Trace
2. Barton
3. Jim Beam
4. Bernheim
5. Early Times
6. Four Roses
7. Heaven Hill
8. Maker's Mark
9. Wild Turkey
10. Jack Daniel
11. George A. Dickel
12. Smith Bowman
13. Tuthilltown

Micro-distilleries in the United States
La micro-distillerie aux États-Unis

The phenomenon of craft and micro-distilleries provides further evidence of the boundless creativity that has always characterized the world of whisky. This is a product that throughout its long history, has never lost sight of its ancestral roots, while still managing to ceaselessly renew itself. And if nobody has any firm idea of what whisky has in store for us over the next ten years, it is a sure bet that it has many more great decades ahead of it.

Le phénomène des craft et des micro-distilleries est un témoignage actuel du bouillonnement créatif qui anime depuis toujours le monde du whisky. Un produit qui, au long de son histoire, a su garder son ancrage ancestral tout en se renouvelant au fil des époques. Et si personne ne saurait deviner ce que nous prépare le whisky dans dix ans, il y a fort à parier qu'il a encore de très beaux jours devant lui.

Cellar Notes

Notes de cave

During tastings, complete your cellar notes based on the example, below.
Voici un exemple de fiche-type à remplir au fil de vos dégustations.

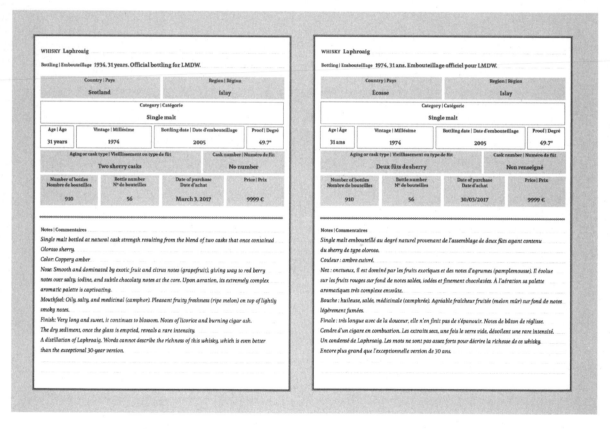

WHISKY **Laphroaig**

Bottling | Embouteillage 1934. 31 years. Official bottling for LMDW.

Country	Pays	Region	Région
Scotland	Islay

Category	Catégorie
Single malt

Age	Âge	Vintage	Millésime	Bottling date	Date d'embouteillage	Proof	Degré
31 years	1974	2005	49.7°

Aging or cask type	Vieillissement ou type de fût		Cask number	Numéro de fût
Two sherry casks	No number

Number of bottles Nombre de bouteilles	Bottle number N° de bouteilles	Date of purchase Date d'achat	Price	Prix
910	56	March 3, 2017	9999 €

Notes | Commentaires

Single malt bottled at natural cask strength resulting from the blend of two casks that once contained Oloroso sherry.

Color: Coppery amber

Nose: Smooth and dominated by exotic fruit and citrus notes (grapefruit), giving way to red berry notes over salty, iodine, and subtle chocolaty notes at the core. Upon aeration, its extremely complex aromatic palette is captivating.

Mouthfeel: Oily, salty, and medicinal (camphor). Pleasant fruity freshness (ripe melon) on top of lightly smoky notes.

Finish: Very long and sweet, it continues to blossom. Notes of licorice and burning cigar ash.

The dry sediment, once the glass is emptied, reveals a rare intensity.

A distillation of Laphroaig. Words cannot describe the richness of this whisky, which is even better than the exceptional 30-year version.

WHISKY **Laphroaig**

Bottling | Embouteillage 1974. 31 ans. Embouteillage officiel pour LMDW.

Country	Pays	Region	Région
Écosse	Islay

Category	Catégorie
Single malt

Age	Âge	Vintage	Millésime	Bottling date	Date d'embouteillage	Proof	Degré
31 ans	1974	2005	49.7°

Aging or cask type	Vieillissement ou type de fût		Cask number	Numéro de fût
Deux fûts de sherry	Non renseigné

Number of bottles Nombre de bouteilles	Bottle number N° de bouteilles	Date of purchase Date d'achat	Price	Prix
910	56	30/03/2017	9999 €

Notes | Commentaires

Single malt embouteillé au degré naturel provenant de l'assemblage de deux fûts ayant contenu du sherry de type oloroso.

Couleur : ambre cuivré.

Nez : onctueux, il est dominé par les fruits exotiques et des notes d'agrumes (pamplemousse). Il évolue sur les fruits rouges sur fond de notes salées, iodées et finement chocolatées. À l'aération sa palette aromatiques très complexe envoûte.

Bouche : huileuse, salée, médicinale (camphrée). Agréable fraîcheur fruitée (melon mûr) sur fond de notes légèrement fumées.

Finale : très longue avec de la douceur, elle n'en finit pas de s'épanouir. Notes de bâton de réglisse. Cendre d'un cigare en combustion. Les extraits secs, une fois le verre vide, dévoilent une rare intensité.

Un condensé de Laphroaig. Les mots ne sont pas assez forts pour décrire la richesse de ce whisky. Encore plus grand que l'exceptionnelle version de 30 ans.

WHISKY ....

Bottling | Embouteillage ....

Country	Pays	Region	Région

Category	Catégorie

Age	Âge	Vintage	Millésime	Bottling date	Date d'embouteillage	Proof	Degré

Aging or cask type	Vieillissement ou type de fût	Cask number	Numéro de fût

Number of bottles Nombre de bouteilles	Bottle number Nº de bouteilles	Date of purchase Date d'achat	Price	Prix

Notes | Commentaires ....

WHISKY

Bottling | Embouteillage

Country	Pays	Region	Région

Category | Catégorie

Age	Âge	Vintage	Millésime	Bottling date	Date d'embouteillage	Proof	Degré

Aging or cask type	Vieillissement ou type de fût	Cask number	Numéro de fût

Number of bottles Nombre de bouteilles	Bottle number N° de bouteilles	Date of purchase Date d'achat	Price	Prix

Notes | Commentaires

WHISKY ....

Bottling | Embouteillage ....

Country	Pays	Region	Région

Category	Catégorie

Age	Âge	Vintage	Millésime	Bottling date	Date d'embouteillage	Proof	Degré

Aging or cask type	Vieillissement ou type de fût	Cask number	Numéro de fût

Number of bottles Nombre de bouteilles	Bottle number N° de bouteilles	Date of purchase Date d'achat	Price	Prix

◇◇◇

Notes | Commentaires ....

WHISKY ....

Bottling | Embouteillage ....

Country	Pays	Region	Région

Category	Catégorie

Age	Âge	Vintage	Millésime	Bottling date	Date d'embouteillage	Proof	Degré

Aging or cask type	Vieillissement ou type de fût	Cask number	Numéro de fût

Number of bottles Nombre de bouteilles	Bottle number N° de bouteilles	Date of purchase Date d'achat	Price	Prix

Notes | Commentaires ....

WHISKY ....

Bottling | Embouteillage ....

Country	Pays	Region	Région

Category	Catégorie

Age	Âge	Vintage	Millésime	Bottling date	Date d'embouteillage	Proof	Degré

Aging or cask type	Vieillissement ou type de fût	Cask number	Numéro de fût

Number of bottles Nombre de bouteilles	Bottle number N° de bouteilles	Date of purchase Date d'achat	Price	Prix

Notes | Commentaires ....

WHISKY ....

Bottling | Embouteillage ....

Country | Pays	Region | Région

Category | Catégorie

Age | Âge	Vintage | Millésime	Bottling date | Date d'embouteillage	Proof | Degré

Aging or cask type | Vieillissement ou type de fût	Cask number | Numéro de fût

Number of bottles Nombre de bouteilles	Bottle number N° de bouteilles	Date of purchase Date d'achat	Price | Prix

Notes | Commentaires ....

WHISKY ....

Bottling | Embouteillage ....

Country	Pays	Region	Région

Category	Catégorie

Age	Âge	Vintage	Millésime	Bottling date	Date d'embouteillage	Proof	Degré

Aging or cask type	Vieillissement ou type de fût	Cask number	Numéro de fût

Number of bottles Nombre de bouteilles	Bottle number N° de bouteilles	Date of purchase Date d'achat	Price	Prix

Notes | Commentaires ....

WHISKY

Bottling | Embouteillage

Country	Pays	Region	Région

Category | Catégorie

Age	Âge	Vintage	Millésime	Bottling date	Date d'embouteillage	Proof	Degré

Aging or cask type | Vieillissement ou type de fût | **Cask number | Numéro de fût**

Number of bottles Nombre de bouteilles	Bottle number N° de bouteilles	Date of purchase Date d'achat	Price	Prix

Notes | Commentaires

WHISKY .....

Bottling | Embouteillage .....

Country	Pays	Region	Région

Category | Catégorie

Age	Âge	Vintage	Millésime	Bottling date	Date d'embouteillage	Proof	Degré

Aging or cask type	Vieillissement ou type de fût	Cask number	Numéro de fût

Number of bottles Nombre de bouteilles	Bottle number N° de bouteilles	Date of purchase Date d'achat	Price	Prix

Notes | Commentaires .....

WHISKY

Bottling | Embouteillage

Country	Pays	Region	Région

Category | Catégorie

Age	Âge	Vintage	Millésime	Bottling date	Date d'embouteillage	Proof	Degré

Aging or cask type	Vieillissement ou type de fût	Cask number	Numéro de fût

Number of bottles Nombre de bouteilles	Bottle number Nº de bouteilles	Date of purchase Date d'achat	Price	Prix

Notes | Commentaires

WHISKY ....

Bottling | Embouteillage ....

Country	Pays	Region	Région

Category	Catégorie

Age	Âge	Vintage	Millésime	Bottling date	Date d'embouteillage	Proof	Degré

Aging or cask type	Vieillissement ou type de fût	Cask number	Numéro de fût

Number of bottles Nombre de bouteilles	Bottle number N° de bouteilles	Date of purchase Date d'achat	Price	Prix

Notes | Commentaires ....

WHISKY ....

Bottling | Embouteillage ....

Country	Pays	Region	Région

Category | Catégorie

Age	Âge	Vintage	Millésime	Bottling date	Date d'embouteillage	Proof	Degré

Aging or cask type	Vieillissement ou type de fût	Cask number	Numéro de fût

Number of bottles Nombre de bouteilles	Bottle number N° de bouteilles	Date of purchase Date d'achat	Price	Prix

◇◇

Notes | Commentaires ....

WHISKY ....

Bottling | Embouteillage ....

Country	Pays	Region	Région

Category | Catégorie

Age	Âge	Vintage	Millésime	Bottling date	Date d'embouteillage	Proof	Degré

Aging or cask type	Vieillissement ou type de fût	Cask number	Numéro de fût

Number of bottles Nombre de bouteilles	Bottle number N° de bouteilles	Date of purchase Date d'achat	Price	Prix

Notes | Commentaires ....

WHISKY ....

Bottling | Embouteillage ....

Country	Pays	Region	Région

Category	Catégorie

Age	Âge	Vintage	Millésime	Bottling date	Date d'embouteillage	Proof	Degré

Aging or cask type	Vieillissement ou type de fût	Cask number	Numéro de fût

Number of bottles Nombre de bouteilles	Bottle number N° de bouteilles	Date of purchase Date d'achat	Price	Prix

Notes | Commentaires ....

WHISKY ....

Bottling | Embouteillage ....

Country	Pays	Region	Région

Category	Catégorie

Age	Âge	Vintage	Millésime	Bottling date	Date d'embouteillage	Proof	Degré

Aging or cask type	Vieillissement ou type de fût	Cask number	Numéro de fût

Number of bottles Nombre de bouteilles	Bottle number N° de bouteilles	Date of purchase Date d'achat	Price	Prix

Notes | Commentaires ....

WHISKY ....

Bottling | Embouteillage ....

Country	Pays	Region	Région

Category	Catégorie

Age	Âge	Vintage	Millésime	Bottling date	Date d'embouteillage	Proof	Degré

Aging or cask type	Vieillissement ou type de fût	Cask number	Numéro de fût

Number of bottles Nombre de bouteilles	Bottle number N° de bouteilles	Date of purchase Date d'achat	Price	Prix

Notes | Commentaires ....

WHISKY ....

Bottling | Embouteillage ....

Country	Pays	Region	Région

Category	Catégorie

Age	Âge	Vintage	Millésime	Bottling date	Date d'embouteillage	Proof	Degré

Aging or cask type	Vieillissement ou type de fût	Cask number	Numéro de fût

Number of bottles Nombre de bouteilles	Bottle number N° de bouteilles	Date of purchase Date d'achat	Price	Prix

Notes | Commentaires ....

WHISKY ....

Bottling | Embouteillage ....

Country	Pays	Region	Région

Category	Catégorie

Age	Âge	Vintage	Millésime	Bottling date	Date d'embouteillage	Proof	Degré

Aging or cask type	Vieillissement ou type de fût	Cask number	Numéro de fût

Number of bottles Nombre de bouteilles	Bottle number N° de bouteilles	Date of purchase Date d'achat	Price	Prix

Notes | Commentaires ....

WHISKY ....

Bottling | Embouteillage ....

Country	Pays	Region	Région

Category	Catégorie

Age	Âge	Vintage	Millésime	Bottling date	Date d'embouteillage	Proof	Degré

Aging or cask type	Vieillissement ou type de fût	Cask number	Numéro de fût

Number of bottles Nombre de bouteilles	Bottle number N° de bouteilles	Date of purchase Date d'achat	Price	Prix

Notes | Commentaires ....

....

....

....

....

....

....

....

....

....

....

....

....

....

WHISKY

Bottling | Embouteillage

Country	Pays	Region	Région

Category | Catégorie

Age	Âge	Vintage	Millésime	Bottling date	Date d'embouteillage	Proof	Degré

Aging or cask type	Vieillissement ou type de fût	Cask number	Numéro de fût

Number of bottles Nombre de bouteilles	Bottle number N° de bouteilles	Date of purchase Date d'achat	Price	Prix

Notes | Commentaires

WHISKY ....

Bottling | Embouteillage ....

Country	Pays	Region	Région

Category	Catégorie

Age	Âge	Vintage	Millésime	Bottling date	Date d'embouteillage	Proof	Degré

Aging or cask type	Vieillissement ou type de fût	Cask number	Numéro de fût

Number of bottles Nombre de bouteilles	Bottle number N° de bouteilles	Date of purchase Date d'achat	Price	Prix

Notes | Commentaires ....

WHISKY ....

Bottling | Embouteillage ....

Country	Pays	Region	Région

Category | Catégorie

Age	Âge	Vintage	Millésime	Bottling date	Date d'embouteillage	Proof	Degré

Aging or cask type | Vieillissement ou type de fût | **Cask number | Numéro de fût**

Number of bottles Nombre de bouteilles	Bottle number N° de bouteilles	Date of purchase Date d'achat	Price	Prix

◇◇◇

Notes | Commentaires ....

WHISKY ....

Bottling | Embouteillage ....

Country	Pays	Region	Région

Category | Catégorie

Age	Âge	Vintage	Millésime	Bottling date	Date d'embouteillage	Proof	Degré

Aging or cask type | Vieillissement ou type de fût | **Cask number | Numéro de fût**

Number of bottles Nombre de bouteilles	Bottle number N° de bouteilles	Date of purchase Date d'achat	Price	Prix

Notes | Commentaires ....

WHISKY ....

Bottling | Embouteillage ....

Country	Pays	Region	Région

Category | Catégorie

Age	Âge	Vintage	Millésime	Bottling date	Date d'embouteillage	Proof	Degré

Aging or cask type | Vieillissement ou type de fût | **Cask number | Numéro de fût**

Number of bottles Nombre de bouteilles	Bottle number N° de bouteilles	Date of purchase Date d'achat	Price	Prix

Notes | Commentaires ....

WHISKY ....

Bottling | Embouteillage ....

Country	Pays	Region	Région

Category	Catégorie

Age	Âge	Vintage	Millésime	Bottling date	Date d'embouteillage	Proof	Degré

Aging or cask type	Vieillissement ou type de fût	Cask number	Numéro de fût

Number of bottles Nombre de bouteilles	Bottle number N° de bouteilles	Date of purchase Date d'achat	Price	Prix

Notes | Commentaires ....

WHISKY

Bottling | Embouteillage

Country	Pays	Region	Région

Category | Catégorie

Age	Âge	Vintage	Millésime	Bottling date	Date d'embouteillage	Proof	Degré

Aging or cask type | Vieillissement ou type de fût **Cask number | Numéro de fût**

Number of bottles Nombre de bouteilles	Bottle number N° de bouteilles	Date of purchase Date d'achat	Price	Prix

Notes | Commentaires

WHISKY ....

Bottling | Embouteillage ....

Country	Pays	Region	Région

Category	Catégorie

Age	Âge	Vintage	Millésime	Bottling date	Date d'embouteillage	Proof	Degré

Aging or cask type	Vieillissement ou type de fût	Cask number	Numéro de fût

Number of bottles Nombre de bouteilles	Bottle number N° de bouteilles	Date of purchase Date d'achat	Price	Prix

Notes | Commentaires ....

WHISKY

Bottling | Embouteillage

Country	Pays	Region	Région

Category | Catégorie

Age	Âge	Vintage	Millésime	Bottling date	Date d'embouteillage	Proof	Degré

Aging or cask type	Vieillissement ou type de fût	Cask number	Numéro de fût

Number of bottles Nombre de bouteilles	Bottle number N° de bouteilles	Date of purchase Date d'achat	Price	Prix

Notes | Commentaires

WHISKY ....

Bottling | Embouteillage ....

Country	Pays	Region	Région

Category | Catégorie

Age	Âge	Vintage	Millésime	Bottling date	Date d'embouteillage	Proof	Degré

Aging or cask type | Vieillissement ou type de fût | **Cask number | Numéro de fût**

Number of bottles Nombre de bouteilles	Bottle number N° de bouteilles	Date of purchase Date d'achat	Price	Prix

Notes | Commentaires ....

WHISKY..

Bottling | Embouteillage..

Country	Pays	Region	Région

Category	Catégorie

Age	Âge	Vintage	Millésime	Bottling date	Date d'embouteillage	Proof	Degré

Aging or cask type	Vieillissement ou type de fût	Cask number	Numéro de fût

Number of bottles Nombre de bouteilles	Bottle number N° de bouteilles	Date of purchase Date d'achat	Price	Prix

Notes | Commentaires...

WHISKY ....

Bottling | Embouteillage ....

Country	Pays	Region	Région

Category	Catégorie

Age	Âge	Vintage	Millésime	Bottling date	Date d'embouteillage	Proof	Degré

Aging or cask type	Vieillissement ou type de fût	Cask number	Numéro de fût

Number of bottles Nombre de bouteilles	Bottle number Nº de bouteilles	Date of purchase Date d'achat	Price	Prix

Notes | Commentaires ....

....

....

....

....

....

....

....

....

....

....

WHISKY..

Bottling | Embouteillage...

Country	Pays	Region	Région

Category | Catégorie

Age	Âge	Vintage	Millésime	Bottling date	Date d'embouteillage	Proof	Degré

Aging or cask type | Vieillissement ou type de fût | **Cask number | Numéro de fût**

Number of bottles Nombre de bouteilles	Bottle number N° de bouteilles	Date of purchase Date d'achat	Price	Prix

Notes | Commentaires..

WHISKY

Bottling | Embouteillage

Country	Pays	Region	Région

Category | Catégorie

Age	Âge	Vintage	Millésime	Bottling date	Date d'embouteillage	Proof	Degré

Aging or cask type | Vieillissement ou type de fût | **Cask number | Numéro de fût**

Number of bottles Nombre de bouteilles	Bottle number Nº de bouteilles	Date of purchase Date d'achat	Price	Prix

Notes | Commentaires

WHISKY

Bottling | Embouteillage

Country	Pays	Region	Région

Category | Catégorie

Age	Âge	Vintage	Millésime	Bottling date	Date d'embouteillage	Proof	Degré

Aging or cask type | Vieillissement ou type de fût | **Cask number | Numéro de fût**

Number of bottles Nombre de bouteilles	Bottle number N° de bouteilles	Date of purchase Date d'achat	Price	Prix

Notes | Commentaires

WHISKY

Bottling | Embouteillage

Country	Pays	Region	Région

Category | Catégorie

Age	Âge	Vintage	Millésime	Bottling date	Date d'embouteillage	Proof	Degré

Aging or cask type	Vieillissement ou type de fût	Cask number	Numéro de fût

Number of bottles Nombre de bouteilles	Bottle number Nº de bouteilles	Date of purchase Date d'achat	Price	Prix

Notes | Commentaires

WHISKY ....

Bottling | Embouteillage ....

Country	Pays	Region	Région

Category	Catégorie

Age	Âge	Vintage	Millésime	Bottling date	Date d'embouteillage	Proof	Degré

Aging or cask type	Vieillissement ou type de fût	Cask number	Numéro de fût

Number of bottles Nombre de bouteilles	Bottle number N° de bouteilles	Date of purchase Date d'achat	Price	Prix

Notes | Commentaires ....

WHISKY ....

Bottling | Embouteillage ....

Country	Pays	Region	Région

Category	Catégorie

Age	Âge	Vintage	Millésime	Bottling date	Date d'embouteillage	Proof	Degré

Aging or cask type	Vieillissement ou type de fût	Cask number	Numéro de fût

Number of bottles Nombre de bouteilles	Bottle number N° de bouteilles	Date of purchase Date d'achat	Price	Prix

Notes | Commentaires ....

WHISKY ....

Bottling | Embouteillage ....

Country	Pays	Region	Région

Category | Catégorie

Age	Âge	Vintage	Millésime	Bottling date	Date d'embouteillage	Proof	Degré

Aging or cask type	Vieillissement ou type de fût	Cask number	Numéro de fût

Number of bottles Nombre de bouteilles	Bottle number N° de bouteilles	Date of purchase Date d'achat	Price	Prix

Notes | Commentaires ....

WHISKY ....

Bottling | Embouteillage ....

Country	Pays	Region	Région

Category | Catégorie

Age	Âge	Vintage	Millésime	Bottling date	Date d'embouteillage	Proof	Degré

Aging or cask type | Vieillissement ou type de fût | **Cask number | Numéro de fût**

Number of bottles Nombre de bouteilles	Bottle number N° de bouteilles	Date of purchase Date d'achat	Price	Prix

Notes | Commentaires ....

WHISKY

Bottling | Embouteillage

Country	Pays	Region	Région

Category | Catégorie

Age	Âge	Vintage	Millésime	Bottling date	Date d'embouteillage	Proof	Degré

Aging or cask type	Vieillissement ou type de fût	Cask number	Numéro de fût

Number of bottles Nombre de bouteilles	Bottle number N° de bouteilles	Date of purchase Date d'achat	Price	Prix

Notes | Commentaires

WHISKY ....

Bottling | Embouteillage ....

Country	Pays	Region	Région

Category | Catégorie

Age	Âge	Vintage	Millésime	Bottling date	Date d'embouteillage	Proof	Degré

Aging or cask type | Vieillissement ou type de fût | **Cask number | Numéro de fût**

Number of bottles Nombre de bouteilles	Bottle number N° de bouteilles	Date of purchase Date d'achat	Price	Prix

⬦⬦

Notes | Commentaires ....

WHISKY ....

Bottling | Embouteillage ....

Country	Pays	Region	Région

Category | Catégorie

Age	Âge	Vintage	Millésime	Bottling date	Date d'embouteillage	Proof	Degré

Aging or cask type	Vieillissement ou type de fût	Cask number	Numéro de fût

Number of bottles Nombre de bouteilles	Bottle number Nº de bouteilles	Date of purchase Date d'achat	Price	Prix

Notes | Commentaires ....

WHISKY ....

Bottling | Embouteillage ....

Country	Pays	Region	Région

Category	Catégorie

Age	Âge	Vintage	Millésime	Bottling date	Date d'embouteillage	Proof	Degré

Aging or cask type	Vieillissement ou type de fût	Cask number	Numéro de fût

Number of bottles Nombre de bouteilles	Bottle number N° de bouteilles	Date of purchase Date d'achat	Price	Prix

Notes | Commentaires ....

WHISKY ....

Bottling | Embouteillage ....

Country	Pays	Region	Région

Category | Catégorie

Age	Âge	Vintage	Millésime	Bottling date	Date d'embouteillage	Proof	Degré

Aging or cask type | Vieillissement ou type de fût | **Cask number | Numéro de fût**

Number of bottles Nombre de bouteilles	Bottle number N° de bouteilles	Date of purchase Date d'achat	Price	Prix

Notes | Commentaires ....

WHISKY ....

Bottling | Embouteillage ....

Country	Pays	Region	Région

Category	Catégorie

Age	Âge	Vintage	Millésime	Bottling date	Date d'embouteillage	Proof	Degré

Aging or cask type	Vieillissement ou type de fût	Cask number	Numéro de fût

Number of bottles Nombre de bouteilles	Bottle number N° de bouteilles	Date of purchase Date d'achat	Price	Prix

Notes | Commentaires ....

WHISKY..

Bottling | Embouteillage...

Country	Pays	Region	Région

Category | Catégorie

Age	Âge	Vintage	Millésime	Bottling date	Date d'embouteillage	Proof	Degré

Aging or cask type | Vieillissement ou type de fût | **Cask number | Numéro de fût**

Number of bottles Nombre de bouteilles	Bottle number N° de bouteilles	Date of purchase Date d'achat	Price	Prix

Notes | Commentaires...

WHISKY ....

Bottling | Embouteillage ....

Country	Pays	Region	Région

Category	Catégorie

Age	Âge	Vintage	Millésime	Bottling date	Date d'embouteillage	Proof	Degré

Aging or cask type	Vieillissement ou type de fût	Cask number	Numéro de fût

Number of bottles Nombre de bouteilles	Bottle number N° de bouteilles	Date of purchase Date d'achat	Price	Prix

Notes | Commentaires ....

WHISKY

Bottling | Embouteillage

Country	Pays	Region	Région

Category	Catégorie

Age	Âge	Vintage	Millésime	Bottling date	Date d'embouteillage	Proof	Degré

Aging or cask type	Vieillissement ou type de fût	Cask number	Numéro de fût

Number of bottles Nombre de bouteilles	Bottle number N° de bouteilles	Date of purchase Date d'achat	Price	Prix

Notes | Commentaires

WHISKY

Bottling | Embouteillage

Country	Pays	Region	Région

Category | Catégorie

Age	Âge	Vintage	Millésime	Bottling date	Date d'embouteillage	Proof	Degré

Aging or cask type | Vieillissement ou type de fût | **Cask number | Numéro de fût**

Number of bottles Nombre de bouteilles	Bottle number N° de bouteilles	Date of purchase Date d'achat	Price	Prix

Notes | Commentaires

WHISKY

Bottling | Embouteillage

Country	Pays	Region	Région

Category	Catégorie

Age	Âge	Vintage	Millésime	Bottling date	Date d'embouteillage	Proof	Degré

Aging or cask type	Vieillissement ou type de fût	Cask number	Numéro de fût

Number of bottles Nombre de bouteilles	Bottle number N° de bouteilles	Date of purchase Date d'achat	Price	Prix

Notes | Commentaires

WHISKY ....

Bottling | Embouteillage ....

Country	Pays	Region	Région

Category	Catégorie

Age	Âge	Vintage	Millésime	Bottling date	Date d'embouteillage	Proof	Degré

Aging or cask type	Vieillissement ou type de fût	Cask number	Numéro de fût

Number of bottles Nombre de bouteilles	Bottle number N° de bouteilles	Date of purchase Date d'achat	Price	Prix

Notes | Commentaires ....

WHISKY ....

Bottling | Embouteillage ....

Country	Pays	Region	Région

Category	Catégorie

Age	Âge	Vintage	Millésime	Bottling date	Date d'embouteillage	Proof	Degré

Aging or cask type	Vieillissement ou type de fût	Cask number	Numéro de fût

Number of bottles Nombre de bouteilles	Bottle number N° de bouteilles	Date of purchase Date d'achat	Price	Prix

Notes | Commentaires ....

WHISKY ....

Bottling | Embouteillage ....

Country	Pays	Region	Région

Category	Catégorie

Age	Âge	Vintage	Millésime	Bottling date	Date d'embouteillage	Proof	Degré

Aging or cask type	Vieillissement ou type de fût	Cask number	Numéro de fût

Number of bottles Nombre de bouteilles	Bottle number Nº de bouteilles	Date of purchase Date d'achat	Price	Prix

Notes | Commentaires ....

WHISKY

Bottling | Embouteillage

Country	Pays	Region	Région

Category | Catégorie

Age	Âge	Vintage	Millésime	Bottling date	Date d'embouteillage	Proof	Degré

Aging or cask type	Vieillissement ou type de fût	Cask number	Numéro de fût

Number of bottles Nombre de bouteilles	Bottle number N° de bouteilles	Date of purchase Date d'achat	Price	Prix

Notes | Commentaires

WHISKY ....

Bottling | Embouteillage ....

Country	Pays	Region	Région

Category | Catégorie

Age	Âge	Vintage	Millésime	Bottling date	Date d'embouteillage	Proof	Degré

Aging or cask type	Vieillissement ou type de fût	Cask number	Numéro de fût

Number of bottles Nombre de bouteilles	Bottle number N° de bouteilles	Date of purchase Date d'achat	Price	Prix

✕✕

Notes | Commentaires ....

WHISKY ....

Bottling | Embouteillage ....

Country	Pays	Region	Région

Category	Catégorie

Age	Âge	Vintage	Millésime	Bottling date	Date d'embouteillage	Proof	Degré

Aging or cask type	Vieillissement ou type de fût	Cask number	Numéro de fût

Number of bottles Nombre de bouteilles	Bottle number N° de bouteilles	Date of purchase Date d'achat	Price	Prix

Notes | Commentaires ....

WHISKY ....

Bottling | Embouteillage ....

Country	Pays	Region	Région

Category | Catégorie

Age	Âge	Vintage	Millésime	Bottling date	Date d'embouteillage	Proof	Degré

Aging or cask type | Vieillissement ou type de fût | **Cask number | Numéro de fût**

Number of bottles Nombre de bouteilles	Bottle number N° de bouteilles	Date of purchase Date d'achat	Price	Prix

Notes | Commentaires ....

WHISKY

Bottling | Embouteillage

Country	Pays	Region	Région

Category	Catégorie

Age	Âge	Vintage	Millésime	Bottling date	Date d'embouteillage	Proof	Degré

Aging or cask type	Vieillissement ou type de fût	Cask number	Numéro de fût

Number of bottles Nombre de bouteilles	Bottle number N° de bouteilles	Date of purchase Date d'achat	Price	Prix

Notes | Commentaires

WHISKY ....

Bottling | Embouteillage ....

Country	Pays	Region	Région

Category | Catégorie

Age	Âge	Vintage	Millésime	Bottling date	Date d'embouteillage	Proof	Degré

Aging or cask type	Vieillissement ou type de fût	Cask number	Numéro de fût

Number of bottles Nombre de bouteilles	Bottle number N° de bouteilles	Date of purchase Date d'achat	Price	Prix

Notes | Commentaires ....

WHISKY

Bottling | Embouteillage

Country	Pays	Region	Région

Category | Catégorie

Age	Âge	Vintage	Millésime	Bottling date	Date d'embouteillage	Proof	Degré

Aging or cask type	Vieillissement ou type de fût	Cask number	Numéro de fût

Number of bottles Nombre de bouteilles	Bottle number N° de bouteilles	Date of purchase Date d'achat	Price	Prix

Notes | Commentaires

WHISKY

Bottling | Embouteillage

Country	Pays	Region	Région

Category | Catégorie

Age	Âge	Vintage	Millésime	Bottling date	Date d'embouteillage	Proof	Degré

Aging or cask type | Vieillissement ou type de fût | **Cask number | Numéro de fût**

Number of bottles Nombre de bouteilles	Bottle number N° de bouteilles	Date of purchase Date d'achat	Price	Prix

Notes | Commentaires

WHISKY...

Bottling | Embouteillage...

Country	Pays	Region	Région

Category	Catégorie

Age	Âge	Vintage	Millésime	Bottling date	Date d'embouteillage	Proof	Degré

Aging or cask type	Vieillissement ou type de fût	Cask number	Numéro de fût

Number of bottles Nombre de bouteilles	Bottle number N° de bouteilles	Date of purchase Date d'achat	Price	Prix

Notes | Commentaires...

WHISKY

Bottling | Embouteillage

Country	Pays	Region	Région

Category | Catégorie

Age	Âge	Vintage	Millésime	Bottling date	Date d'embouteillage	Proof	Degré

Aging or cask type	Vieillissement ou type de fût	Cask number	Numéro de fût

Number of bottles Nombre de bouteilles	Bottle number N° de bouteilles	Date of purchase Date d'achat	Price	Prix

Notes | Commentaires

WHISKY..

Bottling | Embouteillage..

Country	Pays	Region	Région

Category | Catégorie

Age	Âge	Vintage	Millésime	Bottling date	Date d'embouteillage	Proof	Degré

Aging or cask type | Vieillissement ou type de fût | **Cask number | Numéro de fût**

Number of bottles Nombre de bouteilles	Bottle number N° de bouteilles	Date of purchase Date d'achat	Price	Prix

Notes | Commentaires...

WHISKY

Bottling | Embouteillage

Country	Pays	Region	Région

Category | Catégorie

Age	Âge	Vintage	Millésime	Bottling date	Date d'embouteillage	Proof	Degré

Aging or cask type | Vieillissement ou type de fût | **Cask number | Numéro de fût**

Number of bottles Nombre de bouteilles	Bottle number N° de bouteilles	Date of purchase Date d'achat	Price	Prix

Notes | Commentaires

WHISKY ....

Bottling | Embouteillage ....

Country	Pays	Region	Région

Category | Catégorie

Age	Âge	Vintage	Millésime	Bottling date	Date d'embouteillage	Proof	Degré

Aging or cask type | Vieillissement ou type de fût | **Cask number | Numéro de fût**

Number of bottles Nombre de bouteilles	Bottle number N° de bouteilles	Date of purchase Date d'achat	Price	Prix

Notes | Commentaires ....

WHISKY..

Bottling | Embouteillage...

Country | Pays	Region | Région

Category | Catégorie

Age | Âge	Vintage | Millésime	Bottling date | Date d'embouteillage	Proof | Degré

Aging or cask type | Vieillissement ou type de fût	Cask number | Numéro de fût

Number of bottles Nombre de bouteilles	Bottle number N° de bouteilles	Date of purchase Date d'achat	Price | Prix

Notes | Commentaires

WHISKY ....

Bottling | Embouteillage ....

Country	Pays	Region	Région

Category | Catégorie

Age	Âge	Vintage	Millésime	Bottling date	Date d'embouteillage	Proof	Degré

Aging or cask type	Vieillissement ou type de fût	Cask number	Numéro de fût

Number of bottles Nombre de bouteilles	Bottle number N° de bouteilles	Date of purchase Date d'achat	Price	Prix

Notes | Commentaires ....

WHISKY

Bottling | Embouteillage

Country	Pays	Region	Région

Category | Catégorie

Age	Âge	Vintage	Millésime	Bottling date	Date d'embouteillage	Proof	Degré

Aging or cask type | Vieillissement ou type de fût · **Cask number | Numéro de fût**

Number of bottles Nombre de bouteilles	Bottle number Nº de bouteilles	Date of purchase Date d'achat	Price	Prix

Notes | Commentaires

WHISKY

Bottling | Embouteillage

Country	Pays	Region	Région

Category | Catégorie

Age	Âge	Vintage	Millésime	Bottling date	Date d'embouteillage	Proof	Degré

Aging or cask type	Vieillissement ou type de fût	Cask number	Numéro de fût

Number of bottles Nombre de bouteilles	Bottle number N° de bouteilles	Date of purchase Date d'achat	Price	Prix

Notes | Commentaires

WHISKY ....

Bottling | Embouteillage ....

Country	Pays	Region	Région

Category | Catégorie

Age	Âge	Vintage	Millésime	Bottling date	Date d'embouteillage	Proof	Degré

Aging or cask type	Vieillissement ou type de fût	Cask number	Numéro de fût

Number of bottles Nombre de bouteilles	Bottle number N° de bouteilles	Date of purchase Date d'achat	Price	Prix

Notes | Commentaires ....

WHISKY..

Bottling | Embouteillage...

Country	Pays	Region	Région

Category	Catégorie

Age	Âge	Vintage	Millésime	Bottling date	Date d'embouteillage	Proof	Degré

Aging or cask type	Vieillissement ou type de fût	Cask number	Numéro de fût

Number of bottles Nombre de bouteilles	Bottle number N° de bouteilles	Date of purchase Date d'achat	Price	Prix

Notes | Commentaires..

WHISKY

Bottling | Embouteillage

Country	Pays	Region	Région

Category | Catégorie

Age	Âge	Vintage	Millésime	Bottling date	Date d'embouteillage	Proof	Degré

Aging or cask type	Vieillissement ou type de fût	Cask number	Numéro de fût

Number of bottles Nombre de bouteilles	Bottle number N° de bouteilles	Date of purchase Date d'achat	Price	Prix

Notes | Commentaires

WHISKY

Bottling | Embouteillage

Country	Pays	Region	Région

Category | Catégorie

Age	Âge	Vintage	Millésime	Bottling date	Date d'embouteillage	Proof	Degré

Aging or cask type | Vieillissement ou type de fût | **Cask number | Numéro de fût**

Number of bottles Nombre de bouteilles	Bottle number N° de bouteilles	Date of purchase Date d'achat	Price	Prix

Notes | Commentaires

WHISKY ....

Bottling | Embouteillage ....

Country	Pays	Region	Région

Category | Catégorie

Age	Âge	Vintage	Millésime	Bottling date	Date d'embouteillage	Proof	Degré

Aging or cask type | Vieillissement ou type de fût | **Cask number | Numéro de fût**

Number of bottles Nombre de bouteilles	Bottle number Nº de bouteilles	Date of purchase Date d'achat	Price	Prix

✕✕

Notes | Commentaires ....

WHISKY ....

Bottling | Embouteillage ....

Country	Pays	Region	Région

Category | Catégorie

Age	Âge	Vintage	Millésime	Bottling date	Date d'embouteillage	Proof	Degré

Aging or cask type	Vieillissement ou type de fût	Cask number	Numéro de fût

Number of bottles Nombre de bouteilles	Bottle number Nº de bouteilles	Date of purchase Date d'achat	Price	Prix

Notes | Commentaires ....

WHISKY ....

Bottling | Embouteillage ....

Country	Pays	Region	Région

Category | Catégorie

Age	Âge	Vintage	Millésime	Bottling date	Date d'embouteillage	Proof	Degré

Aging or cask type | Vieillissement ou type de fût | **Cask number | Numéro de fût**

Number of bottles Nombre de bouteilles	Bottle number N° de bouteilles	Date of purchase Date d'achat	Price	Prix

Notes | Commentaires ....

WHISKY ....

Bottling | Embouteillage ....

Country	Pays	Region	Région

Category | Catégorie

Age	Âge	Vintage	Millésime	Bottling date	Date d'embouteillage	Proof	Degré

Aging or cask type | Vieillissement ou type de fût | **Cask number | Numéro de fût**

Number of bottles Nombre de bouteilles	Bottle number N° de bouteilles	Date of purchase Date d'achat	Price	Prix

✕✕

Notes | Commentaires ....

WHISKY ....

Bottling | Embouteillage ....

Country	Pays	Region	Région

Category | Catégorie

Age	Âge	Vintage	Millésime	Bottling date	Date d'embouteillage	Proof	Degré

Aging or cask type	Vieillissement ou type de fût	Cask number	Numéro de fût

Number of bottles Nombre de bouteilles	Bottle number N° de bouteilles	Date of purchase Date d'achat	Price	Prix

Notes | Commentaires ....

WHISKY ....

Bottling | Embouteillage ....

Country	Pays	Region	Région

Category	Catégorie

Age	Âge	Vintage	Millésime	Bottling date	Date d'embouteillage	Proof	Degré

Aging or cask type	Vieillissement ou type de fût	Cask number	Numéro de fût

Number of bottles Nombre de bouteilles	Bottle number N° de bouteilles	Date of purchase Date d'achat	Price	Prix

◇◇

Notes | Commentaires ....

WHISKY ....

Bottling | Embouteillage ....

Country	Pays	Region	Région

Category | Catégorie

Age	Âge	Vintage	Millésime	Bottling date	Date d'embouteillage	Proof	Degré

Aging or cask type | Vieillissement ou type de fût | **Cask number | Numéro de fût**

Number of bottles Nombre de bouteilles	Bottle number N° de bouteilles	Date of purchase Date d'achat	Price	Prix

❈❈❈

Notes | Commentaires ....

WHISKY..

Bottling | Embouteillage..

Country	Pays	Region	Région

Category | Catégorie

Age	Âge	Vintage	Millésime	Bottling date	Date d'embouteillage	Proof	Degré

Aging or cask type	Vieillissement ou type de fût	Cask number	Numéro de fût

Number of bottles Nombre de bouteilles	Bottle number N° de bouteilles	Date of purchase Date d'achat	Price	Prix

Notes | Commentaires...

WHISKY ....

Bottling | Embouteillage ....

Country	Pays	Region	Région

Category | Catégorie

Age	Âge	Vintage	Millésime	Bottling date	Date d'embouteillage	Proof	Degré

Aging or cask type | Vieillissement ou type de fût | **Cask number | Numéro de fût**

Number of bottles Nombre de bouteilles	Bottle number N° de bouteilles	Date of purchase Date d'achat	Price	Prix

Notes | Commentaires ....

WHISKY

Bottling | Embouteillage

Country	Pays	Region	Région

Category	Catégorie

Age	Âge	Vintage	Millésime	Bottling date	Date d'embouteillage	Proof	Degré

Aging or cask type	Vieillissement ou type de fût	Cask number	Numéro de fût

Number of bottles Nombre de bouteilles	Bottle number N° de bouteilles	Date of purchase Date d'achat	Price	Prix

Notes | Commentaires

WHISKY

Bottling | Embouteillage

Country	Pays	Region	Région

Category | Catégorie

Age	Âge	Vintage	Millésime	Bottling date	Date d'embouteillage	Proof	Degré

Aging or cask type	Vieillissement ou type de fût	Cask number	Numéro de fût

Number of bottles Nombre de bouteilles	Bottle number N° de bouteilles	Date of purchase Date d'achat	Price	Prix

Notes | Commentaires

WHISKY ....

Bottling | Embouteillage ....

Country	Pays	Region	Région

Category | Catégorie

Age	Âge	Vintage	Millésime	Bottling date	Date d'embouteillage	Proof	Degré

Aging or cask type | Vieillissement ou type de fût | **Cask number | Numéro de fût**

Number of bottles Nombre de bouteilles	Bottle number N° de bouteilles	Date of purchase Date d'achat	Price	Prix

∞∞

Notes | Commentaires ....

WHISKY

Bottling | Embouteillage

Country	Pays	Region	Région

Category	Catégorie

Age	Âge	Vintage	Millésime	Bottling date	Date d'embouteillage	Proof	Degré

Aging or cask type	Vieillissement ou type de fût	Cask number	Numéro de fût

Number of bottles Nombre de bouteilles	Bottle number N° de bouteilles	Date of purchase Date d'achat	Price	Prix

Notes | Commentaires

WHISKY ....

Bottling | Embouteillage ....

Country	Pays	Region	Région

Category	Catégorie

Age	Âge	Vintage	Millésime	Bottling date	Date d'embouteillage	Proof	Degré

Aging or cask type	Vieillissement ou type de fût	Cask number	Numéro de fût

Number of bottles Nombre de bouteilles	Bottle number N° de bouteilles	Date of purchase Date d'achat	Price	Prix

Notes | Commentaires ....

WHISKY

Bottling | Embouteillage

Country	Pays	Region	Région

Category | Catégorie

Age	Âge	Vintage	Millésime	Bottling date	Date d'embouteillage	Proof	Degré

Aging or cask type	Vieillissement ou type de fût	Cask number	Numéro de fût

Number of bottles Nombre de bouteilles	Bottle number N° de bouteilles	Date of purchase Date d'achat	Price	Prix

Notes | Commentaires

WHISKY

Bottling | Embouteillage

Country	Pays	Region	Région

Category | Catégorie

Age	Âge	Vintage	Millésime	Bottling date	Date d'embouteillage	Proof	Degré

Aging or cask type	Vieillissement ou type de fût	Cask number	Numéro de fût

Number of bottles Nombre de bouteilles	Bottle number N° de bouteilles	Date of purchase Date d'achat	Price	Prix

Notes | Commentaires

WHISKY ....

Bottling | Embouteillage ....

Country	Pays	Region	Région

Category | Catégorie

Age	Âge	Vintage	Millésime	Bottling date	Date d'embouteillage	Proof	Degré

Aging or cask type	Vieillissement ou type de fût	Cask number	Numéro de fût

Number of bottles Nombre de bouteilles	Bottle number N° de bouteilles	Date of purchase Date d'achat	Price	Prix

Notes | Commentaires ....

WHISKY

Bottling | Embouteillage

Country	Pays	Region	Région

Category	Catégorie

Age	Âge	Vintage	Millésime	Bottling date	Date d'embouteillage	Proof	Degré

Aging or cask type	Vieillissement ou type de fût	Cask number	Numéro de fût

Number of bottles Nombre de bouteilles	Bottle number N° de bouteilles	Date of purchase Date d'achat	Price	Prix

Notes | Commentaires

WHISKY

Bottling | Embouteillage

Country	Pays	Region	Région

Category	Catégorie

Age	Âge	Vintage	Millésime	Bottling date	Date d'embouteillage	Proof	Degré

Aging or cask type	Vieillissement ou type de fût	Cask number	Numéro de fût

Number of bottles Nombre de bouteilles	Bottle number N° de bouteilles	Date of purchase Date d'achat	Price	Prix

Notes | Commentaires

WHISKY

Bottling | Embouteillage

Country	Pays	Region	Région

Category | Catégorie

Age	Âge	Vintage	Millésime	Bottling date	Date d'embouteillage	Proof	Degré

Aging or cask type | Vieillissement ou type de fût | **Cask number | Numéro de fût**

Number of bottles Nombre de bouteilles	Bottle number N° de bouteilles	Date of purchase Date d'achat	Price	Prix

Notes | Commentaires

WHISKY ....

Bottling | Embouteillage ....

Country	Pays	Region	Région

Category	Catégorie

Age	Âge	Vintage	Millésime	Bottling date	Date d'embouteillage	Proof	Degré

Aging or cask type	Vieillissement ou type de fût	Cask number	Numéro de fût

Number of bottles Nombre de bouteilles	Bottle number N° de bouteilles	Date of purchase Date d'achat	Price	Prix

Notes | Commentaires ....

WHISKY ....

Bottling | Embouteillage ....

Country	Pays	Region	Région

Category	Catégorie

Age	Âge	Vintage	Millésime	Bottling date	Date d'embouteillage	Proof	Degré

Aging or cask type	Vieillissement ou type de fût	Cask number	Numéro de fût

Number of bottles Nombre de bouteilles	Bottle number N° de bouteilles	Date of purchase Date d'achat	Price	Prix

Notes | Commentaires ....

WHISKY ....

Bottling | Embouteillage ....

Country	Pays	Region	Région

Category | Catégorie

Age	Âge	Vintage	Millésime	Bottling date	Date d'embouteillage	Proof	Degré

Aging or cask type	Vieillissement ou type de fût	Cask number	Numéro de fût

Number of bottles Nombre de bouteilles	Bottle number N° de bouteilles	Date of purchase Date d'achat	Price	Prix

Notes | Commentaires ....

WHISKY ....

Bottling | Embouteillage ....

Country	Pays	Region	Région

Category	Catégorie

Age	Âge	Vintage	Millésime	Bottling date	Date d'embouteillage	Proof	Degré

Aging or cask type	Vieillissement ou type de fût	Cask number	Numéro de fût

Number of bottles Nombre de bouteilles	Bottle number N° de bouteilles	Date of purchase Date d'achat	Price	Prix

Notes | Commentaires ....

WHISKY ....

Bottling | Embouteillage ....

Country	Pays	Region	Région

Category | Catégorie

Age	Âge	Vintage	Millésime	Bottling date	Date d'embouteillage	Proof	Degré

Aging or cask type | Vieillissement ou type de fût | **Cask number | Numéro de fût**

Number of bottles Nombre de bouteilles	Bottle number N° de bouteilles	Date of purchase Date d'achat	Price	Prix

✧✧✧

Notes | Commentaires ....

....

....

....

....

....

....

....

....

....

....

....

WHISKY

Bottling | Embouteillage

Country	Pays	Region	Région

Category	Catégorie

Age	Âge	Vintage	Millésime	Bottling date	Date d'embouteillage	Proof	Degré

Aging or cask type	Vieillissement ou type de fût	Cask number	Numéro de fût

Number of bottles Nombre de bouteilles	Bottle number N° de bouteilles	Date of purchase Date d'achat	Price	Prix

Notes | Commentaires

WHISKY ....

Bottling | Embouteillage ....

Country	Pays	Region	Région

Category	Catégorie

Age	Âge	Vintage	Millésime	Bottling date	Date d'embouteillage	Proof	Degré

Aging or cask type	Vieillissement ou type de fût	Cask number	Numéro de fût

Number of bottles Nombre de bouteilles	Bottle number N° de bouteilles	Date of purchase Date d'achat	Price	Prix

Notes | Commentaires ....

WHISKY ....

Bottling | Embouteillage ....

Country	Pays	Region	Région

Category | Catégorie

Age	Âge	Vintage	Millésime	Bottling date	Date d'embouteillage	Proof	Degré

Aging or cask type | Vieillissement ou type de fût | **Cask number | Numéro de fût**

Number of bottles Nombre de bouteilles	Bottle number Nº de bouteilles	Date of purchase Date d'achat	Price	Prix

Notes | Commentaires ....

WHISKY ....

Bottling | Embouteillage ....

Country	Pays	Region	Région

Category	Catégorie

Age	Âge	Vintage	Millésime	Bottling date	Date d'embouteillage	Proof	Degré

Aging or cask type	Vieillissement ou type de fût	Cask number	Numéro de fût

Number of bottles Nombre de bouteilles	Bottle number N° de bouteilles	Date of purchase Date d'achat	Price	Prix

Notes | Commentaires ....

WHISKY ....

Bottling | Embouteillage ....

Country	Pays	Region	Région

Category	Catégorie

Age	Âge	Vintage	Millésime	Bottling date	Date d'embouteillage	Proof	Degré

Aging or cask type	Vieillissement ou type de fût	Cask number	Numéro de fût

Number of bottles Nombre de bouteilles	Bottle number N° de bouteilles	Date of purchase Date d'achat	Price	Prix

Notes | Commentaires ....

WHISKY ....

Bottling | Embouteillage ....

Country	Pays	Region	Région

Category | Catégorie

Age	Âge	Vintage	Millésime	Bottling date	Date d'embouteillage	Proof	Degré

Aging or cask type	Vieillissement ou type de fût	Cask number	Numéro de fût

Number of bottles Nombre de bouteilles	Bottle number N° de bouteilles	Date of purchase Date d'achat	Price	Prix

Notes | Commentaires ....

WHISKY ....

Bottling | Embouteillage ....

Country	Pays	Region	Région

Category	Catégorie

Age	Âge	Vintage	Millésime	Bottling date	Date d'embouteillage	Proof	Degré

Aging or cask type	Vieillissement ou type de fût	Cask number	Numéro de fût

Number of bottles Nombre de bouteilles	Bottle number N° de bouteilles	Date of purchase Date d'achat	Price	Prix

Notes | Commentaires ....

The World's Finest Whiskies

Le Meilleur Du Whisky

Nothing says more about a distillery than its own bottled whiskies. And this is as true for exceptional bottlings that have left their mark on history as it is for classic versions. All are, in their way, standard bearers of a unique kind of expertise.

The goal of the following pages is not to provide an exhaustive list of every distillery; such an approach would become obsolete because dozens of new distilleries open every year. We have chosen, instead, to limit ourselves to just fifty. For each, we mention their most legendary expressions—lauded by experts and sought after worldwide—as well as classic bottles.

To provide breadth to our panorama of the world of whisky, this section concludes with a review of American whiskies and blends, whiskies from around the world, and grain whiskies, as well as craft and micro-distilleries.

Some 500 iconic whiskies from these distilleries are listed, together with nearly 100 great classics that we invite you to discover for yourself. The list is aimed at both the budding enthusiast, keen to build up a cellar with quality whiskies available from merchants, and the experienced collector, who combs specialized online auction websites in the hunt for rare treasures.

Rien n'en dit plus sur une distillerie que ses whiskies. Cela est aussi vrai pour les embouteillages d'exception, qui ont marqué l'histoire de leur empreinte, que pour les versions classiques. Tous sont à leur manière les porte-étendards d'un savoir-faire unique.

Les pages qui suivent n'ont pas pour vocation de dresser une liste exhaustive des distilleries. Une telle démarche rendrait ce livre obsolète dès sa sortie, puisque des dizaines de nouvelles distilleries se créent désormais chaque année.

Nous avons choisi de nous restreindre à cinquante d'entre elles. Pour chacune, vous trouverez les expressions les plus mythiques, adulées des experts et recherchées dans le monde entier, ainsi qu'un embouteillage classique.
Pour dresser un panorama global de l'univers du whisky, cette partie se clôture sur un tour d'horizon des whiskies américains, des blends, des whiskies du monde, des whiskies de grain et des craft et micro-distilleries.

C'est donc à travers plus de 500 références cultes et une centaine de grands classiques que nous vous invitons à découvrir ces distilleries. Une démarche qui s'adresse aussi bien à l'amateur désireux de se constituer une cave à whisky en s'offrant les produits de qualité, disponibles chez les cavistes, qu'au collectionneur aguerri, qui égrène les sites d'enchères spécialisés à la recherche de la perle rare.

1 — **ABERLOUR | 1829 | Scotland/Écosse | Speyside | Aberlour**

2

France's bestselling single malt and the pride and joy of the Pernod Ricard group. Aberlour is especially famous for its wonderfully opulent and moreish sherry-cask versions. The expressions aged in bourbon barrels, while rarer, are no less remarkable for their balance and mildness. The richly mellow older years reveal exotic fruit notes that are the hallmark of the very best. A peerless single malt and a true blue-chip Speyside.

Single malt le plus vendu en France et fleuron du groupe Pernod Ricard, Aberlour est surtout réputé pour ses versions sherry cask (vieillies en fût de xérès) très riches et gourmandes. Plus rares, les expressions vieillies en fût de bourbon se révèlent également remarquables d'équilibre et de douceur. Encore plus onctueux, les vieux millésimes dévoilent des notes de fruits exotiques qui sont la marque de fabrique des plus grands. Un single malt incontournable qui est l'une des valeurs les plus sûres du Speyside.

Great whiskies | Les grands whiskies

3 — ABERLOUR 25 years 1964 OB, 43%, 75cl
ABERLOUR GLENLIVET 8 years 1965 OB, 50%, 75cl
ABERLOUR 1967 OB, 47.7%, 70cl
ABERLOUR 31 years 1970 OB, 56.1%, 70cl
ABERLOUR 30 years 1975 OB, 48.9%, 70cl
ABERLOUR 1976 OB, 43%, 70cl
ABERLOUR 25 years 1980 OB, 51.1%, 70cl
ABERLOUR 14 years Double Cask Matured OB, 58.2%, 70cl
ABERLOUR 12 years A'Bunadh Sterling Silver Label OB, 58.7%, 70cl
ABERLOUR GLENLIVET 8 years OB, 50%, 75cl

The classic | Le classique

4 — ABERLOUR A'Bunadh OB, 61.1%, 70cl

The distilleries are listed in alphabetical order.

Information for each distillery includes:

1–Distillery name | Year established–Year closed (if applicable) | Country | Region | Name of whiskies produced (most bear the name of the distillery, but several expressions are sometimes released, and each one is given a different name). A "†" symbol indicates distilleries that are no longer in operation.

2–A history of the distillery's products: The aromas specific to each distillery, their development over the years, the finest vintages. A unique guide, essential for all who want to create a whisky cellar.

3–The ten finest whiskies: The vast majority are no longer available through "traditional channels," but they represent the best whisky bottled by a distillery

Les distilleries sont classées par ordre alphabétique.

Pour chaque distillerie est indiqué :

1–Son nom | son année de création – son année de fermeture s'il y a lieu | son pays | sa région | le nom des whiskies qu'elle produit (la plupart du temps, le whisky porte le nom de la distillerie, mais il n'est pas rare qu'une distillerie produise plusieurs expressions sous différentes appellations). La "†" indique que la distillerie est fermée.

2–Une histoire de ses produits. Les arômes spécifiques à chaque distillerie, leurs évolutions au fil des années, les meilleurs millésimes... Un guide inédit, indispensable pour quiconque souhaite se doter d'une cave à whisky.

3–Ses dix whiskies les plus cultes. La grande majorité d'entre eux ne sont plus disponibles dans le

during the course of its existence. If you ever have the chance to acquire a bottle, or simply to sip a dram, be aware that you are partaking in a piece of history. Certain recently established distilleries will have manufactured fewer than ten whiskies. To be fair to these distilleries, we have selected a larger number of their classic bottles. Lastly, when a product is shown in bold, it means that it is more than just a great whisky—it is truly legendary!

4–The classic product: Featured in the distillery's permanent range, a classic is readily available and is often reasonably priced. It offers the ideal introduction to a distillery, to help you decide whether or not to explore it further. For certain distilleries, too recent to have made ten great whiskies, we list several classics with very different profiles in order to provide a broad selection. Lastly, for obvious reasons, you will not find any classic bottles by distilleries that are no longer operational; an asterisk appears after the name of such distilleries.

The abbreviation "OB" indicates that the whisky is an official bottling. For whiskies bottled by a wholesaler, the name of the independent bottler is given.

Because the same reference may vary according to when it was bottled, a rotation period is sometimes included on the label. It is an indication of the date the whisky was put into circulation. Some specific rotations are highly sought-after by aficionados.

« circuit classique », mais ils représentent ce que la distillerie a embouteillé de meilleur au cours de son existence. Si vous avez l'occasion de vous en procurer une bouteille, ou simplement d'en déguster un dram, sachez que vous vous tenez en présence d'une page d'histoire ! Certaines distilleries, encore jeunes, en compteront moins de dix. Pour leur rendre justice, nous avons sélectionné davantage d'embouteillages classiques. Enfin, lorsqu'un produit est mis en avant en gras, c'est qu'il a dépassé le stade du grand whisky : il s'agit d'un whisky de légende !

4–Le produit classique. Issu de la gamme permanente de chaque distillerie, le classique est aisément accessible et souvent bon marché. C'est la porte d'entrée indispensable par laquelle on découvre une distillerie. Celle qui donne ou non envie d'aller plus loin. Pour certaines distilleries, encore trop jeunes pour avoir dix grands whiskies, nous avons recensé plusieurs classiques, ayant chacun un profil bien différent pour laisser un large choix à l'amateur. Enfin, pour des raisons évidentes, vous ne trouverez aucun embouteillage classique pour les distilleries fermées.

Pour chacun de ces whiskies, il sera précisé « OB » lorsqu'il s'agit d'un embouteillage officiel. Dans le cas d'un embouteillage de négoce, le nom de l'embouteilleur indépendant sera indiqué.

Puisqu'une même référence peut varier au fil des embouteillages, vous pourrez parfois lire la période de « rotation ». Elle donne une indication sur la date de mise en circulation du whisky. Certaines rotations spécifiques sont extrêmement courues des amateurs.

ABERLOUR | 1829 | Scotland/Écosse | Speyside | Aberlour

France's bestselling single malt and the pride and joy of the Pernod Ricard group, Aberlour is especially famous for its wonderfully opulent and moreish sherry-cask versions. The expressions aged in bourbon barrels, while rarer, are no less remarkable for their balance and mildness. The richly mellow older years reveal exotic fruit notes that are the hallmark of the very best. A peerless single malt and a true blue-chip Speyside.

Single malt le plus vendu en France et fleuron du groupe Pernod Ricard, Aberlour est surtout réputé pour ses versions sherry cask (vieillies en fût de xérès) très riches et gourmandes. Plus rares, les expressions vieillies en fût de bourbon se révèlent également remarquables d'équilibre et de douceur. Encore plus onctueux, les vieux millésimes dévoilent des notes de fruits exotiques qui sont la marque de fabrique des plus grands. Un single malt incontournable qui est l'une des valeurs les plus sûres du Speyside.

Great whiskies | Les grands whiskies
ABERLOUR 25 years 1964 OB, 43%, 75cl
ABERLOUR GLENLIVET 8 years 1965 OB, 50%, 75cl
ABERLOUR 1967 OB, 47.7%, 70cl
ABERLOUR 31 years 1970 OB, 56.1%, 70cl
ABERLOUR 30 years 1975 OB, 48.9%, 70cl
ABERLOUR 1976 OB, 43%, 70cl
ABERLOUR 25 years 1980 OB, 51.1%, 70cl
ABERLOUR 14 years Double Cask Matured OB, 58.2%, 70cl
ABERLOUR 12 years A'Bunadh Sterling Silver Label OB, 58.7%, 70cl
ABERLOUR GLENLIVET 8 years OB, 50%, 75cl

The classic | Le classique
ABERLOUR A'Bunadh OB, 61.1%, 70cl

AMRUT | 1948 | India/Inde | Karnataka | Amrut

If Indian whisky was considered whisky according to European Union legislation, India would be the world's largest producer. It has to be said that Amrut, the first 100% Indian single malt, is every bit as good as a top Scottish single malt. Aged in a tropical climate, Amrut offers young, fruity, and peaty cask-strength expressions as well as a host of marvelously composed limited editions, such as the Intermediate Sherry. Its oldest whisky, Greedy Angels, with an age ranging between 8 and 12 years, presents a maturity worthy of the most venerable Speyside.

Si l'Indian whisky était considéré comme du whisky au sens de la réglementation communautaire, il ferait de l'Inde le premier producteur mondial. En revanche, Amrut, premier single malt 100% indien, n'a rien à envier aux plus grands single malts écossais. Vieilli en climat tropical, Amrut propose en plus de jeunes versions fruitées, tourbées et bruts de fût, une multitude de séries limitées de très grande facture tel l'Intermediate Sherry. Son plus vieux whisky, le Greedy Angels, dont l'âge oscille entre 8 et 12 ans, fait preuve d'une maturité digne des plus vieux Speyside.

Great whiskies | Les grands whiskies
AMRUT 12 years Greedy Angels – 60 years LMDW OB, 60%, 70cl
AMRUT 10 years Greedy Angels OB, 46.61%, 75cl
AMRUT 100 Peated Single Cask Trilogy OB, 57.1%, 70cl
AMRUT Bourbon Single Cask Trilogy OB, 62.8%, 70cl
AMRUT Cask Strength OB, 63.8%, 70cl
AMRUT Double Cask OB, 46%, 70cl
AMRUT Kadhambam OB, 50%, 70cl
AMRUT Portonova OB, 62.1%, 70cl
AMRUT Sherry Matured OB, 57.1%, 70cl
AMRUT Spectrum OB, 50%, 70cl

The classic | Le classique
AMRUT Fusion OB, 50%, 70cl

ARDBEG | 1815 | Scotland/Écosse | Islay | Ardbeg, Kildalton

Inimitable in style, this especially peaty single malt figures in the pantheon of many a whisky connoisseur. Harmonizing perfectly with its sherry cask, its softness and mineral notes make it delightfully drinkable, despite an impressively high phenol level. If collectors remain particularly keen on the more august Ardbegs, notably from the 1960s and 1970s, it is its gloriously rustic 10-year-old versions that have elevated it to the rank of a cult brand. Part of the LVMH portfolio, this single malt is well on the way to becoming a genuine luxury label in its own right.

Ce single malt très tourbé au style inimitable s'inscrit au panthéon du whisky de bon nombre de connaisseurs. S'accommodant parfaitement du sherry, sa douceur et sa minéralité le rendent accessible et particulièrement charmeur malgré un niveau de phénols très élevé. Si les vieux Ardbeg sont très prisés des collectionneurs, notamment les millésimes des années 1960/70, ce sont les anciennes versions de 10 ans très rustiques qui l'ont élevé au rang de marque culte. Un single malt en passe de devenir au sein du portefeuille de LVMH une véritable marque de luxe.

Great whiskies | Les grands whiskies
ARDBEG 1967 Pale Oloroso – Signatory Vintage, 53.7%, 70cl
ARDBEG 1967 – Signatory Vintage, 52.2%, 70cl
ARDBEG 32 years 1967 Old Malt Cask Director's Cut – D. Laing, 49%, 70cl
ARDBEG 1973 Single Cask OB, 49.5%, 70cl
ARDBEG 1974 Provenance OB, 55.6%, 70cl
ARDBEG 25 years 1975 Old Malt Cask – D. Laing, 50%, 75cl
ARDBEG 25 years Lord of the Isles OB, 46%, 70cl
ARDBEG 24 years – Cadenhead, 54.4%, 75cl
ARDBEG 10 years Black Label Clear Glass – Spirit Import OB, 40%, 70cl
ARDBEG Corryvreckan OB, 57.1%, 70cl

The classic | Le classique
ARDBEG Uigeadail OB, 54.2%, 70cl

ARRAN | 1995 | Scotland/Écosse | Isle of Arran | Arran

In this day of micro- and craft distilleries, Arran appears as a veritable ancestral figure. Although the circle of those in the know is growing year by year, its single malt still hovers somewhat under the radar. Under the tongue, the fullness and leathery notes of the sherry-cask varieties offer a contrast with the freshness and vanilla and woody character of those aged in bourbon barrels. On the other hand, all the expressions feel equally mellow and possess a flavorsome quality, as with the peaty Arran named Machrie Moor and many others, all finished in masterly fashion.

À l'ère des craft et des micro-distilleries, Arran fait véritablement figure d'ancêtre. Et même si d'année en année, le cercle des amateurs ne cesse de s'agrandir, son single malt demeure encore très confidentiel. À la dégustation, l'onctuosité et les notes de cuir des versions sherry cask contrastent avec la fraîcheur et le caractère boisé vanillé des versions vieillies en fût de bourbon. En revanche, toutes les expressions affichent une douceur et un caractère gourmand remarquables y compris l'Arran tourbé baptisé Machrie Moor et les nombreux affinages tout en maîtrise.

Great whiskies | Les grands whiskies
ARRAN 20 years 1995 – 60 years LMDW OB, 50.4%, 70cl
ARRAN 2005 Sherry Single Cask LMDW OB, 57.8%, 70cl
ARRAN 21st Anniversary OB, 52.6%, 70cl

The classics | Les classiques
ARRAN 18 years OB, 46%, 70cl
ARRAN 14 years OB, 46%, 70cl
ARRAN 12 years Cask Strength – Batch 6 OB, 52.4%, 70cl
ARRAN 10 years OB, 46%, 70cl
ARRAN The Amarone Cask Finish OB, 50%, 70cl
ARRAN The Bothy Quarter Cask OB, 55.2%, 70cl
ARRAN The Sauternes Cask Finish OB, 50%, 70cl

AUCHENTOSHAN | 1823 | Scotland/Écosse | Lowlands | Auchentoshan

Fluctuating between fruity and floral notes, Auchentoshan represents the prototype Lowland single malt, distinguished from other Scottish single malts by being triple distilled, like an Irish single pot still. Of great complexity, the oldest, dating from the 1950s and 1960s, have blossomed into remarkable ripe and exotic fruit notes of consummate finesse. Over the last few years, the sherry-aged expressions and a wide range of finishings have unveiled an even more flavorful facet of what is an admirably versatile single malt.

―――

Oscillant entre notes fruitées et florales, Auchentoshan est l'archétype du single malt des Lowlands. Il se distingue des autres single malts écossais par une triple distillation chère aux single pot stills irlandais. D'une grande complexité, les plus vieilles expressions des années 1950/60 révèlent également des notes de fruits mûrs et exotiques remarquables de précision. Depuis quelques années les versions vieillies en fût de sherry et différents affinages ont permis de dévoiler une facette plus gourmande de ce single malt très versatile.

Great whiskies | Les grands whiskies
AUCHENTOSHAN 50 years 1957 OB, 49.1%, 70cl
AUCHENTOSHAN 1962 OB, 40.2%, 70cl
AUCHENTOSHAN 40 years 1965 OB, 41.6%, 70cl
AUCHENTOSHAN 31 years 1966. 43.3%, 70cl
AUCHENTOSHAN 44 years 1966 OB, 40.9%, 70cl
AUCHENTOSHAN 1975 Bourbon Cask Matured OB, 46.9%, 70cl
AUCHENTOSHAN 2001 Artist Over 10 Years – LMDW, 54.6%, 70cl
AUCHENTOSHAN 18 years OB, 43%, 75cl
AUCHENTOSHAN 17 years Claret Finish OB, 51%, 70cl
AUCHENTOSHAN 16 years First Fill Bourbon Barrel OB, 53.7%, 70cl

The classic | Le classique
AUCHENTOSHAN 21 years OB, 43%, 70cl

BALBLAIR | 1790 | Scotland/Écosse | Highlands | Balblair

Like a large number of single malts before it, Balblair became known through classic trade varieties, in particular a few old sherry-cask expressions sold by the independent bottler Gordon & MacPhail. The current owner, International Beverage, has striven to reveal another facet of its personality with bourbon-barrel whiskies marked by juicy pear, peach, and apricot notes. When it reverts to tradition, the distillery also offers some remarkable sherry-aged first-fill single casks.

―――

Comme bon nombre de single malts avant lui, Balblair s'est fait connaître par des versions de négoce d'anthologie notamment quelques vieux millésimes sherry cask de l'embouteilleur indépendant Gordon & MacPhail. L'actuel propriétaire, International Beverage, a permis de dévoiler une autre facette de sa personnalité à travers des versions millésimées vieillies en fût de bourbon marquées par des notes de poire juteuse, de pêche et d'abricot. Renouant avec la tradition, la distillerie propose également de remarquables single casks vieillis en fût de sherry de premier remplissage.

Great whiskies | Les grands whiskies
BALBLAIR 18 years 1964 Connoisseurs Choice – Gordon & MacPhail, 40%, 75cl
BALBLAIR 40 years 1965 Anniversary Selection – Single Malt of Scotland, 47.7%, 70cl
BALBLAIR 38 years 1966 Limited Edition OB, 44%, 70cl
BALBLAIR 1969 OB, 55%, 70cl
BALBLAIR 1973 Private Collection – Gordon & MacPhail, 45%, 70cl
BALBLAIR 1973 – Gordon & MacPhail, 53%, 70cl
BALBLAIR 21 years 1975 Dumpy Cask Strength – Signatory Vintage, 56.5%, 70cl
BALBLAIR 1992 Peaty OB, 61%, 70cl
BALBLAIR 35 years Limited Edition OB, 44.2%, 70cl
BALBLAIR 33 years OB, 45.4%, 75cl
BALBLAIR 10 years – Gordon & MacPhail, 57%, 75cl

The classic | Le classique
BALBLAIR 1999 OB, 46%, 70cl

BALVENIE | 1892 | Scotland/Écosse | Speyside | Balvenie (The)

Mellow and malty, this single malt, with its characteristic beeswax notes, represents the epitome of classicism. In the early 2000s, under the auspices its owner, the family firm of William Grant & Sons, a version finished in casks that had contained a single Islay malt created quite a stir. However, the Balvenie Classic—which appeared in the mid-1980s, in its Armagnac-shaped bottle—and to an even greater extent the series of Vintage Casks of the 1960s and 1970s have really propelled Balvenie to the summit.

Ce single malt à la douceur maltée et aux notes caractéristiques de cire d'abeille fait preuve d'un très grand classicisme. Au début des années 2000, sous la houlette de son propriétaire, la société familiale William Grant & Sons, une version affinée dans des fûts ayant contenu un single malt d'Islay avait fait sensation. Mais c'est le Balvenie Classic, dans son flacon en forme de bouteille d'Armagnac, apparu au milieu des années 1980 et plus encore la série des Vintage Casks des années 1960/70 qui ont permis à Balvenie de s'élever au rang des plus grands.

Great whiskies | Les grands whiskies
BALVENIE (The) 50 years 1952 OB, 44.1%, 70cl
BALVENIE (The) 1961 OB, 49.3%, 70cl
BALVENIE (The) 1968 OB, 51%, 70cl
BALVENIE (The) 1973 OB, 49.7%, 70cl
BALVENIE 15 years 1974 – Signatory Vintage, 57.1%, 75cl
BALVENIE (The) Classic Rotation 1984 OB, 43%, 75cl
BALVENIE (The) 40 years Batch #4 OB, 48.5%, 70cl
BALVENIE (The) 30 years OB, 47.3%, 70cl
BALVENIE (The) 17 years Islay Cask OB, 43%, 70cl
BALVENIE (The) Tun 1509 – Batch 2 OB, 50.3%, 70%

The classic | Le classique
BALVENIE (The) 12 years Single Barrel First Fill OB, 47.8%, 70%

BEN NEVIS | 1825 | Scotland/Écosse | Highlands | Ben Nevis

Owned by the Japanese group Nikka since 1989, this very hardy Scottish single malt borrows the still more accentuated salty and iodine notes from its prestigious Japanese counterpart Yoichi, on the island of Hokkaido. Lauded for some rare single-blended versions resulting from a blend of a single malt and a single grain produced on the same site (as in the other distillery belonging to the Nikka group, Miyagikyo), it is above all the single casks of great aromatic complexity distilled in the 1960s and 1970s that stamp this Highland single malt with the mark of true excellence.

Propriété du groupe japonais Nikka depuis 1989, ce single malt écossais très robuste emprunte à son prestigieux homologue japonais Yoichi, sur l'île d'Hokkaido, des notes iodées et salines encore plus exacerbées. Réputé pour quelques rares versions single blended, résultats de l'assemblage d'un single malt et d'un single grain produits sur le même site (comme l'autre distillerie du groupe Nikka, Miyagikyo), ce sont surtout des single casks d'une grande complexité aromatique distillés dans les années 1960/70 qui font de ce single malt un incontournable des Highlands.

Great whiskies | Les grands whiskies
BEN NEVIS 43 years 1966 The Whisky Fair Platinum Selection – D. Laing, 43.8%, 70cl
BEN NEVIS 34 years 1966 Handbottled OB, 53.7%, 70cl
BEN NEVIS 41 years 1967 Handbottled OB, 49.4%, 70cl
BEN NEVIS 40 years 1967 OB, 43.4%, 70cl
BEN NEVIS 32 years 1971 OB, 45.8%, 70cl
BEN NEVIS 34 years 1975 The Prestonfield Limited Edition – Signatory Vintage, 63%, 70cl
BEN NEVIS 30 years 1975 Cask Strength Collection – Signatory Vintage, 63.9%, 70cl
BEN NEVIS 31 years 1984 – 60 years LMDW OB, 56.4%, 70cl
BEN NEVIS 1990 Artist Over 20 Years – LMDW, 60.8%, 70cl
BEN NEVIS 25 years Mr Taketsuru OB, 61.3%, 70cl

The classic | Le classique
BEN NEVIS 10 years OB, 46%, 70cl

BENRIACH | 1898 | Scotland/Écosse | Speyside | Benriach

Although the concept of vintage does not have much traction in the world of whisky, one is nevertheless left wondering about the peculiar alchemy that must have taken place here in many a bourbon barrel filled in 1976 and bottled in the mid-2000s. In the space of a few months, several single casks of that year bloomed into an exceptional fruity palate of what remains a relatively little-known single malt. Quite apart from these august bottles, Benriach has since revealed its full potential in many experiments and finishings of all kinds, including one of the best peaty whiskies from outside of the Isle of Islay.

———

Si la notion de millésime n'existe pas en matière de whisky, on peut toutefois s'interroger sur l'alchimie qui s'est opérée dans de nombreux fûts de bourbon remplis en 1976 et mis en bouteille au milieu des années 2000. En l'espace de quelques mois, plusieurs single casks de ce millésime ont révélé la dimension fruitée exceptionnelle de ce single malt encore méconnu. Au-delà de ces vieux vintages, Benriach a depuis révélé tout son potentiel à travers de nombreuses expérimentations et affinages en tous genres sans oublier l'une des meilleures versions tourbées en dehors de l'île d'Islay.

Great whiskies | Les grands whiskies
BENRIACH 40 years 1966 OB, 50%, 75cl
BENRIACH 35 years 1966 Rare Reserve – Signatory Vintage, 47.2%, 75cl
BENRIACH 36 years 1968 Limited Edition OB, 46%, 70cl
BENRIACH 1970 OB, 51.2%, 70cl
BENRIACH 40 years 1971 Classic Speyside OB, 49.8%, 70cl
BENRIACH 34 years 1976 Classic Speyside OB, 57.8%, 70cl
BENRIACH 33 years 1976 OB, 51.6%, 70cl
BENRIACH 32 years 1976 OB, 50.3%, 70cl
BENRIACH 1976 OB, 53%, 70cl
BENRIACH 1980 Virgin Oak OB, 46%, 70cl

The classic | Le classique
BENRIACH 10 years OB, 43%, 70cl

BENROMACH | 1898 | Scotland/Écosse | Speyside | Benromach

Once the smallest distillery in Speyside, Benromach languished in the shadow of its prestigious elder cousins, until one day, a century after it was founded, its current owner, independent bottlers Gordon & MacPhail, took it upon themselves to wake the sleeping beauty. Updating the mildly peaty style of pre-World War II Speyside single malts, they paved the way for a truly great single malt whose aromatic richness is epitomized in a few hard-to-find examples from the 1960s and 1970s.

———

Benromach, qui fut pour un temps la plus petite distillerie du Speyside, était restée dans l'ombre de ses prestigieuses aînées jusqu'au jour où son actuel propriétaire, l'embouteilleur indépendant Gordon & MacPhail, décida de relancer cette belle endormie, un siècle tout juste après sa création. En remettant au goût du jour le style légèrement tourbé des single malts du Speyside d'avant la Seconde Guerre mondiale, il permit de révéler un grand single malt dont les quelques rares versions millésimées des années 1960/70 démontrent toute la richesse aromatique.

Great whiskies | Les grands whiskies
BENROMACH 55 years 1949 OB, 42.4%, 70cl
BENROMACH 14 years 1965 Connoisseurs Choice, Black Label for Giacone Import – Gordon & MacPhail, 40%, 70cl
BENROMACH 1968 OB, 45.4%, 70cl
BENROMACH 14 years 1968 Connoisseurs Choice, Gradient Brown Label for Meregalli Import – Gordon & MacPhail, 40%, 75cl
BENROMACH 1969 OB, 43%, 70cl
BENROMACH 1975 OB, 49.9%, 70cl
BENROMACH 1976 OB, 46%, 70cl
BENROMACH 30 years OB, 43%, 70cl
BENROMACH 22 years, Port Wood Finish, OB, 45%, 70cl
BENROMACH 21 years OB, 43%, 70cl

The classic | Le classique
BENROMACH 10 years OB, 43%, 70cl

BOWMORE | 1779 | Scotland/Écosse | Islay | Bowmore

Like its colleagues in the south of Islay, and some rare single malts from Speyside, the Hebrides, and the Orkneys, Bowmore proposes a plethora of now legendary whiskies, in particular a large number aged in bourbon barrels that share the same intense tropical fruit notes, such as Bowmore Bouquet 1966 by the late lamented Italian merchant Samaroli. Bowmore is also one of very few distilleries to offer extreme versions that vouchsafe the unique alchemy between the peat and the sherry, such as the legendary Black Bowmore series.

———

À l'instar de ses consœurs du sud de l'île d'Islay et de quelques rares single malts du Speyside, des Hébrides et des Orcades, Bowmore propose une multitude de versions d'anthologie, notamment un grand nombre de qualités vieillies en fût de bourbon qui ont toutes en commun des notes intenses de fruits tropicaux tel le Bowmore Bouquet 1966 du regretté négociant italien Samaroli. Bowmore est également l'une des seules distilleries à proposer des versions extrêmes permettant d'apprécier l'alchimie unique entre la tourbe et le sherry dont la série mythique des Black Bowmore.

Great whiskies | Les grands whiskies
BOWMORE 1956 OB, 43%, 75cl
BOWMORE 30 years 1964 Black – Edition 2 OB, 50%, 70cl
BOWMORE 1964 Bicentenary OB, 43%, 75cl
BOWMORE 1964 Gold OB, 42.4%, 70cl
BOWMORE 1964 White OB, 42.8%, 70cl
BOWMORE 1966 Bouquet – Samaroli, 53%, 70cl
BOWMORE 37 years 1968 OB, 43.4%, 70cl
BOWMORE 30 years 1972 Rare Reserve – Signatory Vintage, 50.3%, 70cl
BOWMORE 35 years 1970 Cask Strength Collection – Signatory Vintage, 56.6%, 70cl
BOWMORE 30 years Sea Dragon Ceramic Decanter OB, 43%, 70cl

The classic | Le classique
BOWMORE 15 years Darkest OB, 43%, 70cl

BRORA † | 1819–1983 | Scotland/Écosse | Highlands | Brora

The richness and subtlety of this single malt make it a true great, and even the very greatest for a number of whisky buffs. Admittedly, it does not possess the extreme character of certain Islays, but its fillings remain exceptionally remarkable in terms of balance and complexity. Oscillating between medicinal and camphor notes, it also reveals spicy, salty, and smoky savors underpinned by a menthol mellowness. It would be difficult to imagine anything superior to the Rare Malts and the Douglas Laing of the 1970s, not forgetting an exceptional 1972 at Gordon & MacPhail's.

———

La richesse et la subtilité de ce single malt en font l'un des plus grands si ce n'est le plus grand pour quelques inconditionnels. Certes, il ne possède pas le caractère extrême de certains Islay, mais son distillat est en tout point remarquable d'équilibre et de complexité. Oscillant entre notes médicinales et camphrées, il dévoile également des saveurs épicées, salines et fumées le tout soutenu par une douceur mentholée. Dans le genre, difficile de faire mieux que les versions Rares Malts ou Douglas Laing des années 1970, sans oublier un vintage 1972 d'exception chez Gordon & MacPhail.

Great whiskies | Les grands whiskies
BRORA 28 years 1971 Old Malt Cask – D. Laing, 50%, 70cl
BRORA 22 years 1972 Rare Malts OB, 58.7%, 70cl
BRORA 1972 Connoisseurs Choice – Gordon & MacPhail, 40%, 70cl
BRORA 30 years 1973 3rd Release OB, 56.6%, 70cl
BRORA 35 years 1977 11th Release Classic Malts OB, 48.1%, 70cl
BRORA 21 years 1977 Rare Malts OB, 56.9%, 70cl
BRORA 18 years 1981 Old Malt Cask – D. Laing, 50%, 70cl
BRORA 25 years 1982 7th Release OB, 56.3%, 70cl
BRORA 19 years 1982 – Silver Seal, 50%, 70cl
BRORA 30 years 4th Release OB, 56.3%, 70cl
BRORA 30 years 5th Release OB, 55.7%, 70cl

BRUICHLADDICH | 1881 | Scotland/Écosse | Islay | Bruichladdich, Octomore, Port Charlotte

This whisky with a name that is unpronounceable for the layman has long languished in relative anonymity. Things picked up, however, at the beginning of the 2000s, when a former master distiller from Bowmore's, Jim McEwan, arrived in the distillery. In just a few years, its range expanded to dozens of versions, including Port Charlotte and Octomore, which reconciled fans of peatiness and extreme sensations with the rebel Bruichladdich. While this single malt now vies with the most characteristic Islays, more classic versions of the 1960s and 1970s also deserve attention.

Ce whisky au nom imprononçable pour le commun des mortels a longtemps souffert d'un relatif anonymat. Tout s'accélère au début des années 2000 lorsque l'ancien maître distillateur de chez Bowmore, Jim Mc Ewan, débarque à la distillerie. En quelques années la gamme s'étoffe de dizaines de versions, dont Port Charlotte et Octomore, qui réconcilient l'amateur de tourbe et de sensations extrêmes avec la rebelle Bruichladdich. Si ce single malt n'a plus rien à envier au plus typé des Islay, les versions plus classiques des années 1960/70 méritent également le détour.

Great whiskies | Les grands whiskies
BRUICHLADDICH 40 years 1964 OB, 43.1%, 70cl
BRUICHLADDICH 36 years 1965 Legacy No.I OB, 40.6%, 70cl
BRUICHLADDICH 15 years 1965 Ceramic decanter OB 52%, 75cl
BRUICHLADDICH 1967 - Signatory Vintage, 43.3%, 70cl
BRUICHLADDICH 32 years 1967 Signatory Feather Range Limited Edition – Signatory Vintage, 48%, 70cl
BRUICHLADDICH 1970 OB, 44.2%, 70cl
BRUICHLADDICH 36 years 1970 125 Years OB, 40.1%, 70cl
PORT CHARLOTTE PC 5 first release OB, 63.5%, 70cl
OCTOMORE 5 years Edition 02 - 140 ppm OB, 62.5%, 70cl
BRUICHLADDICH Infinity OB, 55.5%, 70cl

The classic | Le classique
BRUICHLADDICH Laddie Islay Barley OB, 50%, 70cl

BUNNAHABHAIN | 1881 | Scotland/Écosse | Islay | Bunnahabhain

Like its cousin Bruichladdich, this Islay was often criticized for a more subtle peaty character than usually found in single malts from the south of the island. The arrival of Moine, a Bunnahabhain very high in phenols, has highlighted a new facet that conforms more closely to accepted ideals on the Isle of Islay. The less peaty styles of the 1960s to 1980s, however, spawned some truly great expressions, in which slightly smoky malted barley is perfectly wedded to the exotic fruit notes of a distillate of admirable finesse.

Tout comme son homologue Bruichladdich, cet Islay a souvent été décrié pour son caractère tourbé moins affirmé que celui des single malts du sud de l'île. L'avènement d'un Bunnahabhain très phénolique, baptisé Moine, a permis de mettre en évidence une nouvelle facette plus conforme aux canons en vigueur sur l'île d'Islay. Pourtant, le style moins tourbé des années 1960/70/80 a donné naissance à de très grandes versions où l'orge maltée légèrement fumée se marie parfaitement aux notes de fruits exotiques d'un distillat d'une très grande finesse.

Great whiskies | Les grands whiskies
BUNNAHABHAIN 35 years 1965 Feis Ile OB, 53.9%, 70cl
BUNNAHABHAIN 35 years 1966 Feis Ile OB, 46.1%, 70cl
BUNNAHABHAIN 35 years 1967 Feis Ile OB, 43.8%, 70cl
BUNNAHABHAIN 43 years 1968 Sherry Butt – The Whiskyman, 46.5%, 70cl
BUNNAHABHAIN 1968 Auld Acquaintance OB, 43.8%, 70cl
BUNNAHABHAIN 1969 - Signatory Vintage, 52.8%, 70cl
BUNNAHABHAIN 36 years 1975 - Joint Bottling LMDW & the Whisky Agency, 56.8%, 70cl
BUNNAHABHAIN 27 years 1978 Cask Strength Collection - Signatory Vintage, 55.6%, 70cl
BUNNAHABHAIN 22 years 1980 OB, 42.3%, 70cl
BUNNAHABHAIN 1988 Artist Over 25 Years – LMDW, 56.3%, 70cl

The classic | Le classique
BUNNAHABHAIN Ceobanagh OB, 46.3%, 70cl

CAOL ILA | 1846 | Scotland/Écosse | Islay | Caol Ila

Caol Ila is, without question, one single malt from the Isle of Islay on which all can agree. Not too smoky, nor too medicinal, nor too saline, it displays sweet almond notes that make it widely accessible. And although there was an excellent official 12-year-old version in the 1980s, Caol Ila acquired its spurs with hundreds of single casks and small batches from independent bottlers. Versions from the 1960s and 1970s, in which peatiness melts into a woody vanilla to give rise to marked coconut notes, also deserve a mention.

———

Caol Ila est sans conteste le plus consensuel des single malts de l'île d'Islay. Ni trop fumé ni trop médicinal, ni trop salin, il possède des notes d'amande douce qui le rendent accessible au plus grand nombre. Et même s'il existait une excellente version officielle de 12 ans dans les années 1980, Caol Ila a acquis ses lettres de noblesse grâce aux centaines de single casks et small batches des embouteilleurs indépendants. Avec une mention toute particulière pour les versions des années 1960/70 où la tourbe se fond au boisé vanillé pour donner naissance à de franches notes de noix de coco.

Great whiskies | Les grands whiskies
CAOL ILA 1965 – Gordon & Macphail, 45.6%, 70cl
CAOL ILA 1966 Centenary Reserve – Gordon & MacPhail, 40%, 70cl
CAOL ILA 1968 White Label – Gordon & MacPhail, 58.5%, 70cl
CAOL ILA 15 years 1969 Gradient Brown Label – Meregalli Import – Gordon & MacPhail, 40%, 75cl
CAOL ILA 32 years 1975 Rare Reserve – Signatory Vintage, 58.4%, 70cl
CAOL ILA 20 years 1975 Rare Malts OB, 61.12%, 75cl
CAOL ILA 26 years 1982 – Berry Bros Retro, 55.4%, 70cl
CAOL ILA 15 years Manager Dram OB, 63%, 70cl
CAOL ILA 15 years Orange Label OB, 57%, 75cl
CAOL ILA 15 years Oval Orange Label – Bulloch Lade & Co, 43%, 75cl

The classic | Le classique
CAOL ILA 18 years OB, 43%, 70cl

CHICHIBU | 2008 | Japan/Japon | Kanto | Chichibu

Few distilleries dare to state the age or year of a single malt less than five years old. And rarer still are those whose single malts feel richer and more complex at three years old than certain versions exceeding ten. Chichibu belongs to this category. Bottled at natural cask strength, Chichibu The First hit the ground running, propelling its creator, Ichiro Akuto, to the rank of a distillation genius. Moreover, be it peaty or not, aged in bourbon barrels or in sherry casks, Chichibu invariably displays the same exceptional maturity.

———

Rares sont les distilleries osant afficher l'âge ou le millésime d'un single malt n'excédant pas 5 ans. Et plus rares encore sont celles dont les single malts se révèlent plus complexes et plus riches à 3 ans que certaines versions de plus de 10 ans. Chichibu appartient à cette catégorie. Embouteillé au degré naturel, le Chichibu The First déchaîna les passions dès son lancement, propulsant son créateur, Ichiro Akuto, au rang de génie de la distillation. Et qu'il soit tourbé ou pas, vieilli en fût de bourbon ou en fût de sherry, Chichibu fait preuve à chaque fois d'une exceptionnelle maturité.

Great whiskies | Les grands whiskies
CHICHIBU 2009 Single Cask OB, 61.7%, 70cl
CHICHIBU 2009 Number One Drinks 10th Anniversary Cask OB, 62.1%, 70cl
CHICHIBU 2009 Peated OB, 62%, 70cl
CHICHIBU 3 years 2009 The Floor Malted OB, 50.5%, 70cl
CHICHIBU 2011 Madeira Hogshead Tay Bak Chiang #2 OB, 61.9%, 70cl
CHICHIBU 2014 Chibidaru OB, 53.5%, 70cl
CHICHIBU 3 years The First OB, 61.8%, 70cl
CHICHIBU Newborn Double Matured OB, 61.3%, 70cl
CHICHIBU On The Way OB, 58.5%, 70cl
CHICHIBU Port Pipe OB, 54.5%, 70cl

The classic | Le classique
CHICHIBU The 2016 Peated OB, 54.5%, 70cl

CLYNELISH | 1968 | Scotland/Écosse | Highlands | Clynelish

Though Clynelish was inaugurated in 1968, several unforgettable versions had in fact been distilled in 1965/1966. These single malts come from Clynelish's first distillery, rechristened Brora in 1975 due to a law prohibiting two distilleries from trading under the same name. All concur that the most exceptional qualities can be found in the peaty expressions from the beginning of the 1970s, originating in the old distillery. If admittedly less peaty, the new Clynelish still remains a single malt of character, in particular certain subtly spiced sherry's cask versions.

———

Inaugurée en 1968, plusieurs versions inoubliables furent pourtant distillées en 1965/66 ! Ces single malts proviennent de la première distillerie de Clynelish, rebaptisée Brora en 1975 en raison d'une loi interdisant à deux distilleries de porter le même nom. Tout le monde s'accorde à dire que les qualités les plus exceptionnelles sont les expressions tourbées du début des années 1970, issues de l'ancienne distillerie. Certes moins tourbé, le nouveau Clynelish n'en reste pas moins un single malt de caractère, notamment certaines versions sherry cask subtilement épicées.

Great whiskies | Les grands whiskies
CLYNELISH 34 years 1972 – Single Malts of Scotland, 50.5%, 70cl
CLYNELISH 1972 Book of Kells – Gordon & MacPhail, 59.4%, 70cl
CLYNELISH 24 years 1972 Rare Malt OB, 61.3%, 70cl
CLYNELISH 33 years 1973 The Prestonfield – Signatory Vintage, 54.3%, 70cl
CLYNELISH 17 years 1981 Manager's Dram OB, 61.8%, 70cl
CLYNELISH 23 years 1965 Nidaba Import – Cadenhead, 51.7%, 75cl
CLYNELISH 24 years Sestante – Cadenhead, 49.4%, 75cl
CLYNELISH 12 years White Label for Edward & Edward OB, 56.9%, 75cl
CLYNELISH 12 years – Gordon & Macphail, 57%, 70cl
CLYNELISH 5 years White Label OB, 43%, 75cl

The classic | Le classique
CLYNELISH 14 years Classic Malts OB, 46%, 70cl

DALMORE | 1839 | Scotland/Écosse | Highlands | Dalmore (The)

Forever associated with the stag antlers emblem, The Dalmore is also closely linked to sherry-cask aging. By employing Matusalem or Apostoles sherry casks with a high sugar content in certain versions, Richard Paterson—the very experienced and acclaimed master blender—has forged a style of exceptional richness. From the highly prestigious Constellation range to the 21-year-old Dalmore and more, the list of its legendary versions grows with each passing year. Existing for several decades now, the classic 12 years is positively mythical.

———

Indissociable de l'emblème du bois de cerf, The Dalmore est également intimement lié au vieillissement en fût de sherry. En intégrant dans certaines versions des fûts de sherry Matusalem ou Apostoles à fort taux de sucre, Richard Paterson, le très réputé et expérimenté Master Blender, a donné naissance à un style d'une exceptionnelle richesse. De la très prestigieuse gamme Constellation en passant par les Dalmore de 21 ans et plus, la liste des versions d'anthologie s'allonge chaque année. Le classique 12 ans qui existe depuis plusieurs décennies permet également d'accéder au mythe.

Great whiskies | Les grands whiskies
DALMORE 33 years 1973 OB, 45%, 70cl
DALMORE 32 years 1974 OB, 52%, 70cl
DALMORE 1981 Matusalem Sherry Finesse OB, 44%, 70cl
DALMORE 1981 Amoroso OB, 42%, 70cl
DALMORE 1990 Bourbon Matured OB, 51.8%, 70cl
DALMORE 20 years 1995 Sauternes Wine Cask – 60 years LMDW OB, 53%, 70cl
DALMORE 40 years OB, 40%, 70cl
DALMORE 35 years OB, 40%, 70cl
DALMORE 20 years OB, 43%, 75cl
DALMORE 12 years, Rotation late 1970s OB, 43%, 75cl

The classic | Le classique
DALMORE 15 years OB, 40%, 70cl

EDRADOUR | 1825 | Scotland/Écosse | Highlands | Ballechin, Edradour

Although Edradour can no longer claim to be the "Smallest Distillery in Scotland," it does possess a pair of small stills that produce a very robust distillate marked by characteristic honeyed notes. Since being bought out in 2002 by independent bottler Signatory Vintage, Edradour has enjoyed a new lease of life. Quite apart from its many finishings in wine casks, Edradour expresses its full potential in first-fill sherry casks. Since 2003, it has offered a very peaty second single malt, Ballechin, which can hold its own against the very best Islay.

Si Edradour n'est plus « The Smallest Distillery in Scotland », elle possède en revanche une paire de petits alambics donnant naissance à un distillat très robuste marqué par des notes miellées caractéristiques. Son rachat en 2002 par l'embouteilleur indépendant Signatory Vintage fait entrer Edradour dans une nouvelle ère. Au-delà des nombreux affinages en fût de vin, Edradour exprime tout son potentiel à travers le vieillissement en fût de sherry de premier remplissage. Depuis 2003, elle propose un deuxième single malt très tourbé, Ballechin, qui n'a rien à envier aux meilleurs Islay.

Great whiskies | Les grands whiskies
EDRADOUR 1973 OB, 53.4%, 70cl
EDRADOUR 24 years 1985 Straight From The Cask – Signatory Vintage, 50.2%, 70cl
EDRADOUR 13 years 1989 Decanter – Signatory Vintage, 59%, 70cl
EDRADOUR 1993 Straight From The Cask – Signatory Vintage, 58.6%, 50cl
EDRADOUR 18 years 1998 Sherry Butt – The Nectar 10th Anniversary, 56.7%, 70cl
EDRADOUR 2003 Artist Over 10 Years – LMDW, 54.6%, 70cl
BALLECHIN 2005 Caroni Cask Finish OB, 57.2%, 70cl
BALLECHIN 11 years 2004 Manzanilla Cask Matured Trilogy OB, 56.1%, 70cl
BALLECHIN # 2 Madeira Matured OB, 46%, 70cl
BALLECHIN # 3 Port Matured – Signatory Vintage, 46%, 70cl

The classic | Le classique
BALLECHIN 10 years OB, 46%, 70cl

GLEN GARIOCH | 1797 | Scotland/Écosse | Highlands | Glen Garioch

Property of the Beam Suntory group, Glen Garioch has always lived in the shadow of other distilleries owned by the American–Japanese giant, in particular Bowmore. Like its bigger brother, it boasts characteristic floral notes. And, just like Bowmore, its distillate reacts wonderfully to sherry-cask aging. Although peatier at its beginnings, Glen Garioch today embraces a less phenolic and fruitier register. Certain peaty sherry-cask versions from the early 1970s have earned it a place among the very greatest.

Propriété du groupe Beam Suntory, Glen Garioch a toujours vécu dans l'ombre des autres distilleries du géant américano-japonais, en particulier Bowmore. Elle possède comme son aînée des notes florales caractéristiques. Et tout comme Bowmore, son distillat s'accommode parfaitement d'un vieillissement en fût de sherry. Plus tourbé à ses débuts, Glen Garioch évolue désormais dans un registre moins phénolique et plus fruité. Certaines versions tourbées vieillies en fût de sherry du début des années 1970 lui ont permis de rentrer dans la cour des très grands.

Great whiskies | Les grands whiskies
GLEN GARIOCH 1971 – Samaroli Limited Edition, 59.6%, 75cl
GLEN GARIOCH 1975 – Samaroli, 57%, 75cl
GLEN GARIOCH 8 years 1984 OB, 43%, 75cl
GLEN GARIOCH 25 years 1990 – Silver Seal, 52.1%, 70cl
GLEN GARIOCH 21 years OB, 43%, 75cl
GLEN GARIOCH 21 years, Rotation 1999 OB, 43%, 70cl
GLEN GARIOCH 15 years, Rotation 2003 OB, 43%, 70cl

The classics | Les classiques
GLEN GARIOCH Founders Reserve 1797 OB, 48%, 70cl
GLEN GARIOCH 15 years Renaissance Chapter One OB, 51.9%, 70cl
GLEN GARIOCH 12 years OB, 48%, 70cl

GLEN GRANT | 1840 | Scotland/Écosse | Speyside | Glen Grant

A veritable Speyside institution, Glen Grant was one of the first distilleries to export its single malt at the beginning of the 1960s. Known to the public at large for its youthful incarnations and NAS (No Age Statement), it is, however, one of the few single malts that can age beyond fifty years, improving continuously. It was afforded its letters of nobility by independent bottler Gordon & MacPhail, which still possesses casks dating from the 1940s to 1960s in its houses. Beyond their woody character, certain sherry-cask versions of older than fifty years reveal heady floral notes.

———

Véritable institution dans le Speyside, Glen Grant fut l'une des premières distilleries à exporter son single malt au début des années 1960. Connue du grand public pour ses versions jeunes et sans mention d'âge, c'est pourtant l'un des rares single malts qui puisse vieillir au-delà de 50 ans tout en continuant à se bonifier. L'embouteilleur indépendant Gordon & MacPhail, qui possède encore dans ses chais des barriques des années 1940/50/60, lui a donné ses lettres de noblesse. Certaines versions sherry cask de plus de 50 ans dévoilent au-delà du boisé des notes onctueuses de fleurs capiteuses.

Great whiskies | Les grands whiskies
GLEN GRANT 1955 Rare Vintage – Gordon & MacPhail, 50%, 70cl
GLEN GRANT 1956 Rare Vintage – Gordon & MacPhail, 46%, 70cl
GLEN GRANT 1958 Rare Vintage – Gordon & MacPhail, 40%, 70cl
GLEN GRANT 10 years 1958 OB, 45%, 75cl
GLEN GRANT 1959 – Gordon & MacPhail, 40%, 70cl
GLEN GRANT 42 years 1964 Decanter – Signatory Vintage, 52.8%, 70cl
GLEN GRANT 40 years 1965 Rare Reserve – Signatory Vintage, 56.8%, 70cl
GLEN GRANT 1965 Rare Vintage – Gordon & MacPhail, 40%, 70cl
GLEN GRANT 1972 – Berry Bros, 46%, 70cl
GLEN GRANT Queen's Jubilee Decanter – Gordon & MacPhail, 42.3%, 70cl

The classic | Le classique
GLEN GRANT 12 years, 43%, 70cl

GLENDRONACH | 1826 | Scotland/Écosse | Speyside | Glendronach

This great Highlands vintage is considered by some specialists as the best single malt in the world. A prizewinner at many international competitions, it has earned plaudits with a 12-year-old Matured in Sherry Cask version, which, with the passing of years, has charmed the palate of many a connoisseur. While the current 12 year is less marked by sherry, other versions, aged 18, 21, and 25 years, perpetuate the tradition. On the other hand, the excellent 15-year-old Revival and some great years in the early 1970s, all aged in Oloroso casks, are becoming endangered species.

———

Ce grand cru des Highlands est considéré par certains spécialistes comme le meilleur single malt au monde. Médaillé dans de nombreux concours internationaux, il s'est fait connaître à travers une version de 12 ans Matured in Sherry Cask qui au fil des années a conquis le palais de nombreux amateurs. Si l'actuel 12 ans est moins marqué par le sherry, d'autres versions de 18, 21 et 25 ans perpétuent la tradition. En revanche l'excellent 15 ans revival et les grands millésimes du début des années 1970, tous vieillis en fûts de sherry oloroso, sont désormais en voie de disparition.

Great whiskies | Les grands whiskies
GLENDRONACH 1957 – Gordon & MacPhail, 40%, 75.7cl
GLENDRONACH 25 years 1968 OB, 43%, 75cl
GLENDRONACH 20 years 1970 – Signatory Vintage, 56%, 75cl
GLENDRONACH 40 years 1972 Oloroso OB, 50.2% 70cl
GLENDRONACH 18 years 1972 Limited Edition OB, 43%, 75cl
GLENDRONACH 1972 OB, 53.3%, 70cl
GLENDRONACH 23 years 1975 Selection M.W. Limited Edition – Signatory Vintage, 46%, 70cl
GLENDRONACH 33 years OB, 40%, 70cl
GLENDRONACH 15 years Revival OB, 46%, 70cl
GLENDRONACH 12 years OB, 43%, 75cl

The classic | Le classique
GLENDRONACH 18 years Allardice OB, 46%, 70cl

GLENFARCLAS | 1836 | Scotland/Écosse | Speyside | Glenfarclas

An independent distillery belonging to the Grant family for more than 130 years, Glenfarclas has been famous for the quality of its sherry cask. Marked by leathery notes and red fruit, its single malt is sometimes compared with that from another distillery located to the east of it, Glendronach. In 2007, the distillery created a sensation with the launch of a collection of forty-three vintages distilled between 1952 and 1994. A 21-year-old version bottled in the mid-1970s for the Italian market is sometimes regarded as one of best the single malts produced to date.

Distillerie indépendante appartenant à la famille Grant depuis plus de 130 ans, Glenfarclas est réputée pour la qualité de ses versions vieillies en fût de sherry. Marqué par des notes de cuir et de fruits rouges, son single malt est parfois comparé à celui d'une autre distillerie située plus à l'est, Glendronach. En 2007 la distillerie avait fait sensation en lançant une collection de 43 millésimes distillés entre 1952 et 1994. Une version de 21 ans embouteillée au milieu des années 1970 pour le marché italien est parfois considérée comme l'un des meilleurs single malts produits à ce jour.

Great whiskies | Les grands whiskies
GLENFARCLAS 50 years 1955 OB, 44.4%, 70cl
GLENFARCLAS 50 years 1956 OB, 50%, 70cl
GLENFARCLAS 40 years 1958 10th Anniversary – Signatory Vintage, 52.8%, 75cl
GLENFARCLAS 1960 The Family Casks OB, 52.4%, 70cl
GLENFARCLAS 1965 The Family Casks OB, 60%, 70cl
GLENFARCLAS 40 years 1968 105 The Family Casks OB, 60%, 70cl
GLENFARCLAS 24 years 1969 Dumpy Bottle – Signatory Vintage, 56.5%, 70cl
GLENFARCLAS 1970 OB, 46%, 70cl
GLENFARCLAS 21 years Square Bottle OB, 51.5%, 75cl
GLENFARCLAS 12 years 86° Proof OB, 43%, 75cl

The classic | Le classique
GLENFARCLAS 105 OB, 60%, 70cl

GLENFIDDICH | 1887 | Scotland/Écosse | Speyside | Glenfiddich

In the early 1960s, Glenfiddich was one of the first distilleries to begin exporting its single malt. Its triangular bottle is not the only attraction of this Scotch, which has belonged to the same family since its foundation. The smoothness of its distillate and the quality of its aging—every Glenfiddich rests a few months before bottling—make it one of the great Speyside classics. As for the Glenfiddich aged 30 and 40 years, they are exceedingly drinkable, as are the two 50-year-old versions and the single casks from the 1970s, much sought after by collectors.

Glenfiddich fut, au début des années 1960, l'une des premières distilleries à exporter son single malt. Sa bouteille triangulaire n'est pas le seul attrait de ce single malt, qui appartient toujours à la même famille depuis sa création. La finesse de son distillat et la qualité de son vieillissement – tous les Glenfiddich reposent quelques mois avant d'être embouteillés – en font l'un des grands classiques du Speyside. Quant aux vieux Glenfiddich de 30 et 40 ans, ils se révèlent très gourmands tout comme les deux versions de 50 ans et les single casks des années 1970, prisés des collectionneurs.

Great whiskies | Les grands whiskies
GLENFIDDICH 1963 OB, 47.6%, 70cl
GLENFIDDICH 1972 OB, 47.1%, 70cl
GLENFIDDICH 34 years 1973 Private Vintage OB, 46.6%, 70cl
GLENFIDDICH 32 years 1974 Private Vintage OB, 47.3%, 70cl
GLENFIDDICH 34 years 1975 Rare Collection OB, 53.4%, 70cl
GLENFIDDICH 31 years 1977 OB, 54.1%, 70cl
GLENFIDDICH 50 years OB, 43%, 75cl
GLENFIDDICH 40 years Rare Collection OB, 41.7%, 70cl
GLENFIDDICH 30 years Silver Stag's Head Decanter OB, 43%, 75cl
GLENFIDDICH 8 years Straight Malt OB, 43%, 75cl

The classic | Le classique
GLENFIDDICH 18 years Ancient OB, 40%, 70cl

GLENLIVET | 1824 | Scotland/Écosse | Speyside | Glenlivet

The history of this great Speyside brand deserves a chapter to itself in the epic of Scotch whisky. After being smuggled for centuries, Glenlivet became the first Highland distillery to obtain an official license for distillation. The reason it features in our roll call of excellence, however, is above all the sophistication and elegance of a very fruity single malt, in particular the 18 year old. And, as with other single malts from the area, Glenlivet improves with age, as demonstrated by vintage versions from the 1940s to 1960s by independent bottler Gordon & MacPhail.

———

L'histoire de ce grand nom du Speyside est intimement liée à l'épopée du scotch whisky. Après des siècles de contrebande, Glenlivet fut en effet la première distillerie des Highlands à obtenir une licence officielle de distillation. Mais si elle figure dans notre palmarès, c'est avant tout pour la finesse et l'élégance de son single malt qui se révèle très fruité, en particulier le 18 ans. Et à l'image d'autres single malts de la région, Glenlivet se bonifie avec l'âge comme le démontrent les versions millésimées des années 1940/50/60 de l'embouteilleur indépendant Gordon & MacPhail.

Great whiskies | Les grands whiskies
GLENLIVET 49 years 1938 Decanter – Gordon & MacPhail, 40%, 75cl
GLENLIVET 1938 Gordon & MacPhail, 40%, 75cl
GLENLIVET 70 years 1940 Generations – Gordon & MacPhail, 45.9%, 20cl
GLENLIVET (The) 1964 Cellar Collection OB, 45.1%, 70cl
GLENLIVET 1965 Single Cask – Gordon & MacPhail, 46%, 70cl
GLENLIVET 27 years 1968 – Signatory Vintage, 48%, 70cl
GLENLIVET 1981 Artist Over 30 Years – LMDW, 49.8%, 70cl
GLENLIVET 50 years LMDW 50th Anniversary – Gordon & MacPhail, 40%, 70cl
GLENLIVET (The) 20 years, Unblended All Malts OB, 45.7%, 75cl
GLENLIVET (The) 12 years, Rotation early 1970s OB, 45.7%, 75cl

The classic | Le classique
GLENLIVET (The) 18 years OB, 43%, 70cl

GLENMORANGIE | 1843 | Scotland/Écosse | Highlands | Glenmorangie

Famous for its large stills, Glenmorangie makes a fine and subtle single malt. Now under French ownership, this whisky, which for a long time was the favorite single malt of the Scots themselves, also gave rise to one of the most important revolutions in aging. In the mid-1990s, Bill Lumsden, then in charge of production, transformed this single malt, until then known for its 10- and 18-year-old versions, by introducing the concept of "finish." Second caskings (finishings) in Tain l'Hermitage or Sauternes have thus marked the history of this ever-innovative distillery.

———

Célèbre pour ses alambics de grande taille, Glenmorangie élabore un single malt fin et subtil. Désormais sous pavillon français, celui qui fut longtemps le single malt préféré des écossais est à l'origine de l'une des principales révolutions en matière de vieillissement. Au milieu des années 1990, Bill Lumsden, en charge de la création, a transformé ce single malt, jusqu'alors connu pour son 10 ans et son 18 ans, en introduisant la notion de « finish ». Les affinages en fût de Tain l'Hermitage ou de Sauternes ont ainsi marqué l'histoire de cette distillerie qui ne cesse d'innover.

Great whiskies | Les grands whiskies
GLENMORANGIE 22 years 1963 Pure Old Highland Malt OB, 43%, 75cl
GLENMORANGIE 22 years 1971 150th Anniversary Limited Edition OB, 43%, 70cl
GLENMORANGIE 1972 Single Barrel OB, 46%, 75cl
GLENMORANGIE 1974 Original OB, 43%, 50cl
GLENMORANGIE 1975 Tain l'Hermitage OB, 46%, 70cl
GLENMORANGIE 18 years 1987 Margaux Finish OB, 46%, 70cl
GLENMORANGIE 30 years OB, 44.3%, 70cl
GLENMORANGIE 10 years Tradition 100 Proof OB, 57.2%, 100cl
GLENMORANGIE Côte de Nuits Finish OB, 43%, 70cl
GLENMORANGIE Pride OB, 56.7%, 100cl

The classic | Le classique
GLENMORANGIE 12 years Nectar d'Or OB, 46%, 70cl

GLENROTHES | 1878 | Scotland/Écosse | Speyside | Glenrothes

Little-known until 1995, Glenrothes emerged from the shadows with the launch of a 15-year-old single malt distilled in 1979 in a revolutionary oval bottle. It very quickly carved out a position on the international market, particularly in Spain. Going beyond its original incarnation, Glenrothes is a rich single malt much appreciated by master blenders, especially certain versions aged in sherry casks. Moreover, like a considerable number of Speyside single malts, Glenrothes improves over time; versions from the 1960s and 1970s are particularly palatable.

Très confidentielle jusqu'en 1995, Glenrothes sort de l'anonymat en lançant sur le marché un single malt de 15 ans distillé en 1979 dans une bouteille de forme ovale révolutionnaire. Très vite Glenrothes s'impose à l'international, notamment en Espagne. Au-delà de son flacon original, Glenrothes est un single malt riche apprécié des Master Blenders, notamment certaines versions vieillies en fût de sherry. Et comme bon nombre de single malts du Speyside, Glenrothes se bonifie avec l'âge : les vieux millésimes des années 1960/70 se révélant particulièrement gourmands.

Great whiskies | Les grands whiskies
GLENROTHES (The) 1968 Extraordinary Cask OB, 41.9%, 70cl
GLENROTHES 31 years 1969 Old Malt Cask – D. Laing, 50%, 70cl
GLENROTHES 1970 – Taste Still Selection, 41.8%, 70cl
GLENROTHES 41 years 1970 Romantique – The Whisky Agency, 47.7%, 70cl
GLENROTHES 1972 Sample Room Restricted Release OB, 43%, 70cl
GLENROTHES 33 years 1972 Limited Release OB, 43%, 75cl
GLENROTHES 33 years 1972 Cask Strength Collection – Signatory Vintage, 56.6%, 70cl
GLENROTHES 25 years 1979, 55.2%, 70cl
GLENROTHES 17 years Sestante Decanter – Gordon & Macphail, 59.5%, 75cl
GLENROTHES (The) John Ramsay Legacy OB, 46.7%, 70cl

The classic | Le classique
GLENROTHES (The) Sherry Cask Reserve OB, 40%, 70cl

HANYU † | 1946–2000 | Japan/Japon | Saitama prefecture | Hanyu

Founded by the grandfather of Ichiro Akuto, the owner of Chichibu, Hanyu is a cult, like other now closed distilleries such as Karuizawa and Port Ellen. Following the dismantling of the distillery in 2004, Ichiro bought up the entire stock produced between 1980 and 2000, and in 2005 launched a first version with a label featuring a playing card: the king of diamonds. This provided the inspiration for a sequel of fifty-four editions, forming a collection comprising a complete pack. The last card, the Joker Monochrome, was launched in 2014. There still remain some barrels of this malt with pronounced woody notes in Ichiro's warehouse.

Fondée par le grand père d'Ichiro Akuto, le propriétaire de Chichibu, Hanyu est culte, au même titre que d'autres distilleries fermées telles Karuizawa ou Port Ellen. Suite au démantèlement de la distillerie en 2004, Ichiro racheta tout le stock produit entre 1980 et 2000 et lança en 2005 une première version avec, en guise d'étiquette, une carte à jouer, le roi de carreau. Ceci lui inspira la suite, une collection constituée de 54 éditions, un jeu complet. La dernière carte, le Joker Monochrome, fut lancée en 2014. Il reste encore quelques fûts de ce malt au boisé prononcé dans les chais d'Ichiro.

Great whiskies | Les grands whiskies
HANYU 1985 Ichiro's Malt OB, 57.1%, 70cl
HANYU 1986 Ace of Diamonds OB, 56.4%, 70cl
HANYU 1986 Ace of Spades OB, 55.7%, 70cl
HANYU 1988 OB, 55.6%, 70cl
HANYU 1988 King of Clubs OB, 58% 70cl
HANYU 1991 Eight of Hearts OB, 56.8%, 70cl
HANYU 2000 The Game OB, 59.4%, 70cl
HANYU The Joker Multi Vintage OB, 57.7% , 70cl
HANYU The Joker Monochrome OB, 54.9%, 70cl
HANYU 15 years Final Vintage OB, 46.5%, 70cl

HIGHLAND PARK | 1798 | Scotland/Écosse | Orkney | Highland Park

Highland Park is unique in more ways than one. The most northern distillery in Scotland, lodged in the middle of an island swept by gales, its rich range of flavors makes it one of the most complete single malts in the world. Marked by floral notes tinged by heather honey and citrus, it presents a mildly smoky finish that delights peat fans. While the 18-year-old Highland Park is reliable, the versions distilled in the late 1950s aged from 17 to 21 years—sometimes bottled cask strength and aged in sherry butts—bloom into a rare complexity.

Highland Park est unique à plus d'un titre. Distillerie la plus septentrionale d'Écosse, au cœur d'une île balayée par les vents marins, sa riche palette aromatique en fait l'un des single malts les plus complets au monde. Marqué par des notes florales, de miel de bruyère et d'agrumes, il possède une finale légèrement fumée qui ravira les amateurs de tourbe. Si le Highland Park 18 ans demeure une valeur sûre, les versions distillées à la fin des années 1950 âgées de 17 à 21 ans, parfois embouteillées au degré naturel et vieillies en fût de sherry, témoignent d'une rare complexité.

Great whiskies | Les grands whiskies
HIGHLAND PARK 30 years 1955 Intertrade Import – Gordon & MacPhail, 53.2%, 75cl
HIGHLAND PARK 18 years 1956 Dumpy OB, 43%, 75cl
HIGHLAND PARK 21 years 1959 Dumpy Bottle Rotation 1980 OB, 43%, 75cl
HIGHLAND PARK 18 years 1960 OB, 43%, 75cl
HIGHLAND PARK 1967 Dumpy Bottling OB, 43%, 70cl
HIGHLAND PARK 1970 OB, 48%, 70cl
HIGHLAND PARK 33 years 1973 Binny's USA – OB, 54.5%, 75cl
HIGHLAND PARK 40 years OB, 48.3%, 70cl
HIGHLAND PARK 17 years Dumpy OB, 43%, 75cl
HIGHLAND PARK 11 years Ferraretto Import OB, 43%, 75cl

The classic | Le classique
HIGHLAND PARK 18 years OB, 43%, 70cl

JURA | 1810 | Scotland/Écosse | Isle of Jura | Jura

Jura is the only distillery on the island from which it takes its name. Under the aegis of master blender Richard Paterson, this traditionally non-peaty single malt aged in bourbon barrels has recently undergone a renaissance. There now exists a singularly peaty version of high quality named Prophecy, as well as sherry-cask expressions and limited series finished in barrels from various sources. Finally, among the most accomplished expressions are certain references from the 1970s that still used the high-quality and increasingly scarce Golden Promise variety of barley.

Jura est la seule distillerie de l'île dont elle porte le nom. Sous la houlette de son Master Blender, Richard Paterson, ce single malt traditionnellement non tourbé et vieilli en fût de bourbon a récemment fait sa révolution. Il existe désormais une version très tourbée de grande qualité baptisée Prophecy, mais aussi des versions sherry cask et des séries limitées affinées dans différents types de fûts. Citons enfin parmi les expressions les plus abouties certaines références des années 1970, qui utilisaient encore la qualité d'orge Golden Promise, désormais en voie de disparition.

Great whiskies | Les grands whiskies
JURA 1974 OB, 44.5%, 70cl
JURA 1975 Port Cask – 60 years LMDW OB, 51.7%, 70cl
JURA 1976 OB, 46%, 70cl
JURA 1977 OB, 46%, 70cl
JURA 1984 OB, 44%, 70cl
JURA 1989 Water OB, 49.6%, 70cl
JURA 40 years OB, 45.1%, 70cl
JURA 36 years OB, 44%, 70cl
JURA 10 years, Cask Strength OB, 57.2%, 70cl
JURA 8 years, Rotation late 1970s OB, 40%, 75cl

The classic | Le classique
JURA Prophecy OB, 46%, 70cl

KARUIZAWA † | 1956–2000 | Japan/Japon | Chubu | Asama, Karuizawa

There are scarcely any superlatives left to describe the Karuizawa phenomenon. Built at the foot of Mount Asama, a still active volcano, whiskies from this distillery, which was dismantled in 2011, are today the object of a veritable cult. Several hundred barrels have been put on the market since 2007, including a large number of single casks, principally sherry, bottled cask strength. The very greatest include the 1967 Cask #6426, the 1968 Cask #6955, and the 1960, of which only forty-one were produced, at an estimated value of $115,000 USD/£90,000 GBP. A word to the wise: a few dozen barrels are still quietly aging in the warehouse.

Les superlatifs manquent pour décrire le phénomène Karuizawa. Construite au pied du mont Asama, volcan encore actif, cette distillerie démantelée en 2011 fait désormais l'objet d'un véritable culte. Plusieurs centaines de fûts ont été commercialisés depuis 2007 dont un grand nombre de single casks, essentiellement des fûts de sherry, embouteillés cask strength. Citons parmi les plus grandes versions le 1967 fût 6426, le 1968 fût 6955 et le vintage 1960, produit à seulement 41 exemplaires, estimé à plus de 100 000 €. Il reste encore quelques dizaines de fûts en vieillissement. Avis aux amateurs.

Great whiskies | Les grands whiskies
KARUIZAWA 1960 OB, 51.8%, 70cl
KARUIZAWA 48 years 1964 OB, 57.7%, 70cl
KARUIZAWA 1965 Japonism Edition – 60 years LMDW OB, 62.41%, 80cl
KARUIZAWA 1965 Cask #8636 OB, 62.6%, 70cl
KARUIZAWA 1967 OB, 58.4%, 70cl
KARUIZAWA 1968 OB, 61.1%, 70cl
KARUIZAWA 1972 OB, 65%, 70cl
KARUIZAWA 1977 Kamiasobi OB, 62.8%, 70cl
KARUIZAWA 31 years 1981 Cask #78 OB, 60.5%, 70cl
KARUIZAWA 28 years 1983 Noh OB, 57.2%, 70cl

KAVALAN | 2006 | Taiwan | Yilan County | Kavalan

In ten short years, Kavalan has risen to become not only one of the best single malts in the world, but also one of greatest malt distilleries remaining in activity. The owner, the family firm of King Car, achieved this feat under the guidance of the eminent consultant Jim Swan. And it was a wise move, because in 2015 Kavalan Vinho Barrique was voted the best whisky in the world. Relying on the very choicest butts, primarily sherry casks, its secret lies in its aging in a tropical climate: in Taiwan a 7-year-old single malt presents the maturity of a 25-year-old Speyside!

En l'espace de 10 ans, Kavalan est non seulement devenu l'un des meilleurs single malts au monde, mais aussi l'une des plus grandes distilleries de malt en activité. Son propriétaire, le groupe familial King Car, s'est donné les moyens en s'offrant les services d'un éminent consultant, Jim Swan. Bien lui en a pris puisqu'en 2015, Kavalan Vinho Barrique est élu meilleur whisky au monde. Misant sur des fûts de tout premier choix, essentiellement des sherry casks, son secret réside dans un vieillissement en climat tropical : à Taiwan, un single malt de 7 ans possède la maturité d'un Speyside de 25 ans !

Great whiskies | Les grands whiskies
KAVALAN Brandy Single Cask OB, 59.4%, 70cl
KAVALAN Distillery Reserve Whisky Live 2015 OB, 54%, 70cl
KAVALAN Peaty Cask – 60 years LMDW OB, 52.4%, 70cl
KAVALAN Solist Sherry Single Cask OB, 57.8%, 70cl
KAVALAN Solist Vinho Barrique OB, 58.6%, 70cl

The classics | Les classiques
KAVALAN Solist Ex-Bourbon Cask OB, 59.4%, 70cl
KAVALAN Solist Fino Sherry Cask OB, 57.8%, 70cl
KAVALAN Solist Port Cask OB, 57.1%, 70cl
KAVALAN Solist Sherry Cask OB, 55.6%, 70cl
KAVALAN Solist Vinho Barrique OB, 57.1%, 70cl

KILCHOMAN | 2005 | Scotland/Écosse | Islay | Kilchoman

Located on the northwest of the Isle of Islay, Kilchoman is one of the most promising distilleries established since 2000. In 2008, the distillery firm started proposing small batches combining a majority of bourbon barrels with a few sherry casks. In 2011, it launched a 100% Islay version, distilled from its own malted barley. The following year, Kilchoman unveiled a 5-year-old version aged in Oloroso casks named after nearby Loch Gorm. In ten years, it has succeeded in imposing its fresh and slightly peaty style. And the best is surely to come.

———

Située au nord-ouest de l'île d'Islay, Kilchoman est l'une des distilleries les plus prometteuses créées après l'an 2000. Cette ferme distillerie propose depuis 2008 de petites cuvées associant une majorité de fûts de bourbon et quelques fûts de sherry. En 2011, elle lance une version 100% Islay, distillée à partir de sa propre orge maltée. L'année suivante, Kilchoman dévoile une version de 5 ans vieillie en fût de sherry oloroso baptisée du nom d'un lac situé à proximité, Loch Gorm. En 10 ans, elle a réussi à imposer son style frais et légèrement tourbé. Et le meilleur est sans doute à venir.

Great whiskies | Les grands whiskies
KILCHOMAN 2009 PX Finish Single Cask LMDW OB, 56%, 70cl
KILCHOMAN 5 years 2011 Caroni Cask Finish – 60 years LMDW OB, 59.4%, 70cl
KILCHOMAN 10th Anniversary OB, 58.2%, 70cl
KILCHOMAN Inaugural Release OB, 46%, 70cl
KILCHOMAN Whisky Live Paris OB, 61.1%, 70cl

The classics | Les classiques
KILCHOMAN 100% Islay Release 7th Edition OB, 50%, 70cl
KILCHOMAN Loch Gorm OB, 46%, 70cl
KILCHOMAN Machir Bay OB, 46%, 70cl
KILCHOMAN Original Cask Strength Release OB, 56.9%, 70cl
KILCHOMAN Sanaig OB, 46%, 70cl

LAGAVULIN | 1816 | Scotland/Écosse | Islay | Lagavulin

In the 1970s, Lagavulin was already selling a 12-year-old version that has since become almost impossible to find, but it was in 1988 that everything changed. Relaunched in the Classic Malts of Scotland range, Lagavulin quickly made a name with its 16-year-old whisky in a unique peaty style. Since then, the fever has continued unabated. And even if other distilleries, in particular its two neighbors Laphroaig and Ardbeg, have since emerged, Lagavulin remains king of the castle. Whether 8, 12, 21, or 25 years old, aged in bourbon barrels or sherry casks, the consistency of Lagavulin is impressive. And that is the hallmark of the very finest.

———

Dans les années 1970, Lagavulin proposait déjà une version de 12 ans devenue quasi-introuvable, mais c'est en 1988 que tout bascule. Relancé au sein de la gamme des Classic Malts of Scotland, Lagavulin impose rapidement ses 16 ans et son style tourbé unique. Depuis cette date, la fièvre n'est jamais retombée. Et même si d'autres distilleries, en particulier ses deux voisines Laphroaig et Ardbeg, ont depuis émergé, Lagavulin reste indétrônable. À 8, 12, 21 ou 25 ans, vieilli en fût de bourbon ou en fût de sherry, Lagavulin impressionne par sa consistance. Sans doute la marque des plus grands.

Great whiskies | Les grands whiskies
LAGAVULIN 37 years 1976 OB, 51%, 70cl
LAGAVULIN 15 years 1979 – The Syndicate's, 59.2%, 70cl
LAGAVULIN 1979 OB, 43%, 70cl
LAGAVULIN 12 years White Label Rot 1979 Montenegro Import OB, 43%, 75cl
LAGAVULIN 1988 – Moon Import, 46%, 70cl
LAGAVULIN 21 years 1991 OB, 52%, 70cl
LAGAVULIN 1995 Islay Jazz Festival OB, 51.9%, 70cl
LAGAVULIN 16 years White Horse Distillers Ltd OB, 43%, 70cl
LAGAVULIN 12 years White Horse Distillers Ltd OB, 43%, 75cl
LAGAVULIN 12 years 13th Release OB, 55.1%, 70cl

The classic | Le classique
LAGAVULIN 16 years OB, 43%, 70cl

LAPHROAIG | 1815 | Scotland/Écosse | Islay | Laphroaig

The Legend of Laphroaig, the title of a book written by one of the preeminent collectors of bottles from this distillery, perfectly captures the place of this single malt in the imaginations of connoisseurs. Long outshone by its youthful neighbor Lagavulin, Laphroaig is characterized in particular by the active malting plant it owns. One version is unanimously hailed: the mythic 10 year. Over time, the camphor and medicinal notes recede before red fruits, in particular in certain sherry-cask expressions, when the notoriously hostile Laphroaig turns into a veritable nectar.

La Légende de Laphroaig, le nom d'un ouvrage écrit par l'un des plus grands collectionneurs de cette distillerie, résume assez bien la place de ce single malt dans l'imaginaire des amateurs. Longtemps dans l'ombre de sa cadette et voisine Lagavulin, Laphroaig se distingue notamment par une aire de maltage toujours en activité. Une version fait généralement l'unanimité, le mythique 10 ans. Avec le temps, le camphre et les notes médicinales font place aux fruits rouges notamment dans certaines versions sherry cask, et le Laphroaig réputé si hostile devient alors un véritable nectar.

Great whiskies | Les grands whiskies
LAPHROAIG 28 years 1967 Dumpy Range – Signatory Vintage, 50.3%, 70cl
LAPHROAIG 1970 – Samaroli, 54%, 75cl
LAPHROAIG 31 years 1974 Sherry Cask OB, 49.7%, 70cl
LAPHROAIG 1976 Vintage OB, 43%, 75cl
LAPHROAIG 10 years Rotation 1979 – Bonfanti Import OB, 43%, 75cl
LAPHROAIG 27 years 1980 Oloroso Cask OB, 57.4%, 70cl
LAPHROAIG 40 years OB, 42.4%, 70cl
LAPHROAIG 30 years OB, 43%, 70cl
LAPHROAIG 15 years, Rotation late 2000s OB, 43%, 70cl
LAPHROAIG 10 years Cask Strength First Edition OB, 57.3%, 70cl

The classic | Le classique
LAPHROAIG 10 years OB, 40%, 70cl

LINKWOOD | 1821 | Scotland/Écosse | Speyside | Linkwood

Located in north Speyside, on the edge of the town of Elgin, Linkwood remains a distillery little known to the general public, though its name is sure to make the ears of connoisseurs prick up. The most glorious versions are those by the independent bottler Gordon & MacPhail, which markets many vintages from the 1940s to the 1970s, as well as a 15 year old that has become a benchmark. If Linkwood appears rich and complex when aged in sherry casks, younger versions—which are consummately elegant—tend to reveal characteristic hazelnut notes.

Située au nord du Speyside en bordure de la ville d'Elgin, Linkwood est une distillerie méconnue du grand public mais dont le nom résonne aux oreilles des amateurs. Les plus belles versions sont celles de l'embouteilleur indépendant Gordon & MacPhail, qui commercialise de nombreuses versions millésimées des années 1940/50/60/70 ainsi qu'une version de 15 ans qui fait généralement référence. Si Linkwood se révèle riche et complexe sous l'influence d'un vieillissement en fût de sherry, les plus jeunes versions, très élégantes, dévoilent des notes caractéristiques de noisette.

Great whiskies | Les grands whiskies
LINKWOOD 1946 Rare Vintage – Gordon & MacPhail, 40%, 70cl
LINKWOOD 12 years 1957 OB, 56.9%, 75cl
LINKWOOD 22 years 1972 Rare Malt OB, 59.3%, 70cl
LINKWOOD 30 years 1974 Rare Malt OB, 54.9%, 70cl
LINKWOOD 23 years 1974 Rare Malt OB, 61.2%, 75cl
LINKWOOD 1985 Artist Over 25 Years – LMDW, 54.7%, 70cl
LINKWOOD 16 years 1997 Single Cask – Gordon & MacPhail, 45%, 70cl
LINKWOOD 45 years Crystal Decanter – Sestante, 40%, 75cl
LINKWOOD 25 years – Sestante, 40%, 75cl
LINKWOOD 12 years, Darma Import OB, 43%, 75cl

The classic | Le classique
LINKWOOD 15 years – Gordon & MacPhail Distillery Labels, 43%, 70cl

LONGMORN | 1893 | Scotland/Écosse | Speyside | Longmorn

Part of the Pernod Ricard portfolio since 2001, Longmorn is far from being a household name. True whisky buffs, on the other hand, have seen the light and regularly place this distillery among their favorites. Once again, it was the independent bottlers who facilitated its breakthrough. Versions from the 1960s and 1970s bottled by Gordon & MacPhail are models of their kind. Like many other Speyside single malts of the first rank, Longmorn reveals exotic fruit notes. Certain sherry-cask versions revel in the bitterness of dark chocolate.

Au sein du portefeuille de Pernod Ricard depuis 2001, Longmorn ne s'est pas encore imposée auprès du grand public. En revanche, les amateurs ne s'y trompent pas, plaçant régulièrement cette distillerie parmi leurs préférées. Une fois encore ce sont les embouteilleurs indépendants qui ont permis à Longmorn d'émerger. Les versions des années 1960/70 embouteillées par Gordon & MacPhail sont des modèles du genre. Comme d'autres très grands single malts du Speyside, Longmorn dévoile des notes de fruits exotiques. Certaines versions sherry cask font également ressortir l'amertume du chocolat noir.

Great whiskies | Les grands whiskies
LONGMORN 43 years 1964 Single Cask – Gordon & MacPhail, 50%, 70cl
LONGMORN 1969 Prestonfield – Signatory Vintage, 43%, 70cl
LONGMORN 1969 Single Cask – Gordon & MacPhail, 50%, 70cl
LONGMORN 39 years 1969 The Whisky Exchange 10th Anniversary – Gordon & MacPhail, 57.7%, 70cl
LONGMORN 25 years 1969 – Gordon & MacPhail, 61.2%, 70cl
LONGMORN 38 years 1971 for Limburg – Gordon & MacPhail, 47.4%, 70cl
LONGMORN 1972 Single Cask – Gordon & MacPhail, 46%, 70cl
LONGMORN 34 years 1972 Single Cask – Gordon & MacPhail, 45%, 70cl
LONGMORN 1973 Cask Strength – Gordon & MacPhail, 54.4%, 70cl
LONGMORN 1974 – Cadenhead, 60.8%, 75cl

The classic | Le classique
LONGMORN 16 years OB, 48%, 70cl

MACALLAN | 1824 | Scotland/Écosse | Speyside | Macallan (The)

In the opinion of Michael Jackson, a great whisky specialist and author of the *Malt Whisky Companion* who passed away in 2007, the 18-year-old sherry-cask Macallan was the best single malt in the world. Nowadays, expressions aged 100% in sherry casks are becoming rare indeed, the majority of the stocks being earmarked for Asia—Taiwan in particular—where they sell like hot cakes. Yet it was in another country, Italy, that the legend was first written. Originally, the majority of the versions from the 1930s to the 1960s—sherry casks for the most part—were intended for the Italian market, and the price for such bottles at auction continues to climb steadily.

Aux yeux de Michael Jackson, grand spécialiste du whisky disparu en 2007, auteur du guide *Malt Whisky Companion*, le Macallan 18 ans sherry cask était le meilleur single malt au monde. De nos jours, les versions âgées 100% sherry se font rares, la plupart des stocks étant réservés à l'Asie, notamment Taiwan qui en raffole. Mais c'est un autre pays, l'Italie, qui a construit le mythe. La plupart des versions des années 1930/40/50/60, en majorité des sherry casks, étaient à l'origine destinées au marché italien, des bouteilles dont la cote ne cesse de grimper dans les ventes aux enchères.

Great whiskies | Les grands whiskies
MACALLAN GLENLIVET 34 years 1937 – Gordon & MacPhail, 43%, 75cl
MACALLAN (The) 1938 Handwritten label with red ribbon OB, 43%, 75cl
MACALLAN (The) 15 years 1947 80° Proof OB, 45.9%, 75cl
MACALLAN (The) 1955 Campbell, Hope & King OB, 45.7%, 75cl
MACALLAN (The) 25 years 1957 Red Ribbon OB, 43%, 75cl
MACALLAN (The) 25 years 1962 Decanter OB, 43%, 75cl
MACALLAN (The) 29 years 1965 – Signatory Vintage, 49%, 70cl
MACALLAN (The) 18 years 1966 OB, 43%, 75cl
MACALLAN (The) 18 years 1979 Gran Reserva OB, 40%, 70cl
MACALLAN (The) 10 years 100 Proof – Giovinetti Import OB, 57%, 75cl

The classic | Le classique
MACALLAN (The) Sienna OB, 43%, 70cl

MIDLETON | 1825 (1975) | Ireland/Irlande | County Cork | Dungourney, Green Spot, Jameson, Midleton, Powers, Redbreast, Yellow Spot

Midleton is an exception in our honors list, as it is the only distillery that does not produce single malts, but rather single pot stills, based on malted and unmalted barley. In 2016, expert Jim Murray was spot on when he ranked Midleton Dair Ghaelach as the third-best whiskey in the world. Midleton impresses with its fruitiness. The finest expressions veer between various fruits: yellow flesh, red berries, and exotic. One of them, Redbreast, has quite rightly been dubbed the "Irish nectar".

Midleton est une exception au sein de notre palmarès. C'est en effet la seule distillerie qui ne produise pas de single malts, mais des single pot stills, élaborés à base d'orge maltée et non maltée. L'expert Jim Murray ne s'y est d'ailleurs pas trompé, classant le Midleton Dair Ghaelach troisième meilleur whisky au monde en 2016. Midleton impressionne par le fruité de ses whiskeys. Les meilleures expressions oscillent en permanence entre les fruits à chair jaune, les fruits rouges et les fruits exotiques. L'un d'entre eux, le Redbreast, est qualifié à juste titre de nectar irlandais.

Great whiskies | Les grands whiskies
DUNGOURNEY 1964 OB, 40%, 70cl
MIDLETON 30 years 1973 OB, 56%, 70cl
MIDLETON 1998 Sherry Cask OB, 59.7%, 70cl
REDBREAST 25 years OB, 53%, 70cl
MIDLETON 25 years OB, 43%, 70cl
REDBREAST 15 years 1st Release OB, 46%, 70cl
JAMESON 15 years Pure Pot Still OB, 40%, 70cl
MIDLETON V.R. 20th Anniversary OB, 53%, 70cl

The classics | Les classiques
REDBREAST 12 years Single Pot Still OB, 40%, 70cl
POWER'S 12 years John Lane Single Pot Still OB, 46%, 70cl
MIDLETON Dair Ghaelach Single Pot Still OB, 57.9%, 70cl

MIYAGIKYO | 1969 | Japan/Japon | Miyagi prefecture | Miyagikyo

Owned by the Nikka group, Miyagikyo remains less in the limelight than its esteemed elder cousin Yoichi. Nonetheless, it shares the same versatile character, which relishes aging in new oak as much as in first-fill sherry casks. But although Miyagikyo has gained favor thanks to some truly top-drawer single casks aged in sherry, the full potential of this distillery is best revealed in the rarer, highly peaty versions. The peatiness is wedded to the fruity notes of the distillate, resulting in chocolaty flavors as well as hints of sweet and savory.

Propriété du groupe Nikka, Miyagikyo est moins réputée que sa prestigieuse aînée Yoichi. Elle partage cependant le même caractère versatile qui s'accommode aussi bien d'un vieillissement en fût de chêne neuf qu'en fût de sherry de premier remplissage. Et même si Miyagikyo s'est fait connaître à travers quelques single casks vieillis en fût de sherry de tout premier plan, ce sont les versions très tourbées plus rares qui révèlent tout le potentiel de cette distillerie. Une tourbe qui, en se mélangeant aux notes fruitées du distillat, donne naissance à des saveurs sucrées, salées et chocolatées.

Great whiskies | Les grands whiskies
MIYAGIKYO 21 years 1986 Single Cask OB, 63%, 70cl
MIYAGIKYO 17 years 1987 Sherry Single Cask OB, 62%, 70cl
MIYAGIKYO 1988 Single Cask OB, 57%, 70cl
MIYAGIKYO 1989 Single Cask OB, 60%, 70cl
MIYAGIKYO 1990 Single Cask OB, 61%, 70cl
MIYAGIKYO 1991 Single Cask OB, 62%, 70cl
MIYAGIKYO 1996 Light Peat Single Cask 42439 OB, 62%, 70cl
MIYAGIKYO 1999 Light Peat Single Cask OB, 61%, 70cl
MIYAGIKYO 2002 Single Cask OB, 62%, 70cl
MIYAGIKYO 12 years 70th Anniversary OB, 58%, 70cl

The classic | Le classique
MIYAGIKYO Single Malt OB, 45%, 70cl

MORTLACH | 1823 | Scotland/Écosse | Speyside | Mortlach

Until 2014 and the launch of an official range composed of NAS versions, one of 18 and the other of 25 years, this robust single malt, which adapts wonderfully to sherry casking, was practically unknown to the public. Once again, it was independent bottler Gordon & MacPhail, specialist in Speyside single malts, that revealed its qualities to connoisseurs. The firm still possesses sherry casks from the 1930s to the 1960s in its warehouses. In 2008, it hit the headlines by marketing fifty-four bottles of 70-year-old Mortlach 1938, the oldest single malt in the world at that time.

Jusqu'en 2014 et le lancement d'une gamme officielle composée de versions sans âge, d'un 18 et d'un 25 ans, ce single malt robuste qui s'accommode à merveille du sherry était quasi inconnu du grand public. Et c'est une nouvelle fois le spécialiste des single malts du Speyside, l'embouteilleur indépendant Gordon & MacPhail, qui le fit connaître auprès des amateurs. Ce dernier possède encore dans ses chais des fûts de sherry des années 1930/40/50/60. En 2008 il fit sensation en lançant sur le marché 54 bouteilles d'un Mortlach 1938 âgé de 70 ans, le plus vieux single malt au monde à l'époque.

Great whiskies | Les grands whiskies
MORTLACH 35 years 1936 OB, 43%, 75cl
MORTLACH 70 years 1938 Generations – Gordon & MacPhail, 46.1%, 70cl
MORTLACH 44 years 1938 Connoisseurs Choice Gradient Brown Label Meregalli Import – Gordon & MacPhail, 40%, 75cl
MORTLACH 75 years 1939 Rare Vintage Crystal Decanter – Gordon & MacPhail, 44.4%, 70cl
MORTLACH 50 years 1939 Rare Vintage Crystal Decanter – Gordon & MacPhail, 40%, 75cl
MORTLACH 1954 – Gordon & MacPhail Rare Vintage, 43%, 70cl
MORTLACH 32 years 1971 Limited Edition OB, 50.1%, 70cl
MORTLACH 1971 – Gordon & MacPhail Rare Vintage, 43%, 70cl
MORTLACH 23 years 1972 Rare Malts OB, 59.4%, 75cl
MORTLACH 1975 Cask Strength Collection – Signatory Vintage, 56.8%, 70cl

The classic | Le classique
MORTLACH 18 years OB, 43. 40%, 50cl

PORT ELLEN † | 1825–1983 | Scotland/Écosse | Islay | Port Ellen

Port Ellen surely constitutes the first myth in the postwar history of single-malt Scotch. When Diageo unveiled a 20-year-old Port Ellen in the Rare Malts range in 1998, the general opinion was that this would be its swan song. Twenty years later and there already exist sixteen limited editions, and all the indications are that the series will not stop there. Oily and highly phenolic, a young Port Ellen less than 20 years old (today virtually impossible to find) is a far cry from the versions that are more than 30 years old, which are launched every year, and which are always very smoky, albeit milder and sweeter.

Port Ellen fut sans doute le tout premier mythe de l'histoire du single malt écossais d'après-guerre. Lorsque Diageo dévoile en 1998 un Port Ellen de 20 ans dans la gamme des Rares Malts, tout le monde pense qu'il s'agit d'un chant du cygne. Vingt ans plus tard nous en sommes déjà à 16 éditions limitées et tout porte à croire que la série ne devrait pas s'arrêter là. Huileux et très phénoliques, les jeunes Port Ellen de moins de 20 ans, désormais quasi-introuvables, n'ont rien à voir avec les versions de plus de 30 ans lancées chaque année toujours très fumées mais plus sages et plus douces.

Great whiskies | Les grands whiskies
PORT ELLEN 16 years 1969 Gradient Brown Label for Meregalli – Gordon & MacPhail, 40%, 75cl
PORT ELLEN 15 years 1969 Celtic Label for Meregalli – Gordon & MacPhail, 64.7%, 75cl
PORT ELLEN 1971 Connoisseurs Choice – Gordon & MacPhail, 40%, 75cl
PORT ELLEN 30 years 1974 Cask Strength Collection – Signatory Vintage, 58.5%, 70cl
PORT ELLEN 22 years 1978 Rare Malt OB, 60.5%, 70cl
PORT ELLEN 1979 – Gordon & MacPhail, 61.1%, 70cl
PORT ELLEN 22 years 1979 1st Release OB, 56.2%, 70cl
PORT ELLEN 25 years 1982 Cask Strength Collection Collectors Edition – Signatory Vintage, 55.7%, 70cl
PORT ELLEN 21 years 1982 Old Malt Cask – D. Laing, 50%, 70cl
PORT ELLEN 30 years 9th Release OB, 57.7%, 70cl

PULTENEY | 1826 | Scotland/Écosse | Highlands | Old Pulteney

Located in the extreme north of Scotland, in the small harbor town of Wick, Pulteney is a single malt that will not leave fans of iodine-rich whisky unmoved. Somewhat ignored by the general public, it nevertheless enjoys a solid reputation with the majority of whisky connoisseurs. The versions aged in Oloroso casks are particularly interesting: marine and iodized notes blend with the mellowness of the sherry to give rise to sweet and savory notes reminiscent of another, mildly saline type of sherry, Manzanilla.

Située à l'extrême nord de l'Ecosse, dans la petite ville portuaire de Wick, Pulteney est un single malt qui ne laissera pas insensible les amateurs de whiskies iodés. Encore méconnu du grand public, il n'en possède pas moins une solide réputation auprès de la plupart des amateurs. Les versions vieillies en fût de sherry oloroso se révèlent particulièrement intéressantes : les notes marines et iodées du whisky se mélangeant à la douceur du sherry, donnant naissance à des notes sucrées salées non sans rappeler un autre type de sherry légèrement salin baptisé Manzanilla.

Great whiskies | Les grands whiskies
OLD PULTENEY 1961 Rare Single Highland Malt – Gordon & MacPhail, 40%, 75cl
OLD PULTENEY 1966 – Gordon & MacPhail, 40%, 70cl
OLD PULTENEY 1968 – Gordon & MacPhail, 46%, 70cl
OLD PULTENEY 20 years 1968 – Gordon & MacPhail, 43%, 75cl
OLD PULTENEY 1969 OB, 56.2%, 70cl
OLD PULTENEY 1974 Rare Vintage – Gordon & MacPhail, 43%, 70cl
OLD PULTENEY 1989 OB, 46%, 70cl
OLD PULTENEY 17 years 1989 Malt Pedigree MW – Signatory Vintage, 59.5%, 70cl
OLD PULTENEY 12 years 2004 Sherry Cask – 60 years LMDW OB, 61.3%, 70cl
OLD PULTENEY 35 years First Release OB, 42.5%, 70cl

The classic | Le classique
OLD PULTENEY 21 years OB, 46%, 70cl

ROSEBANK † | 1840–1993 | Scotland/Écosse | Lowlands | Rosebank

There remain some rare versions of this whisky, often regarded as the greatest in the Lowlands, marketed by independent bottlers and the owner, Diageo. Contrary to common belief, Rosebank needs time to rise to its full potential. Although the younger expressions have a certain charm with their floral and lemony notes, older versions grow in complexity, revealing mild spice and beeswax. Certain Rosebanks of 20 years old and more, distilled in the 1960s, can hold their own against the best Speyside single malts of the same period.

Souvent considéré comme le plus grand des Lowlands, il existe encore quelques rares versions commercialisées par des embouteilleurs indépendants et le propriétaire Diageo. Contrairement aux idées reçues, Rosebank a besoin de temps pour exprimer son potentiel. Si les jeunes expressions ne manquent pas de charme avec leurs notes florales et citronnées, les versions âgées se révèlent plus complexes, dévoilant des épices douces et de la cire d'abeille. Certains Rosebank de 20 ans et plus, distillés dans les années 1960, n'ont rien à envier aux meilleurs single malts du Speyside de la même époque.

Great whiskies | Les grands whiskies
ROSEBANK 30 years 1974 Magnum – Silver Seal, 55.8%, 150cl
ROSEBANK 27 years 1975 Old Malt Cask – D. Laing, 50%, 70cl
ROSEBANK 20 years 1979 Rare Malt OB, 60.3%, 70cl
ROSEBANK 20 years 1981 Rare Malt OB, 62.3%, 70cl
ROSEBANK 25 years 1981 OB, 61.4%, 70cl
ROSEBANK DISTILLERY 21 years OB, 55.1%, 70cl
ROSEBANK 20 years OB, 57%, 75cl
ROSEBANK 20 years Distillers Agency Ltd OB, 57%, 75cl
ROSEBANK 15 years Unblended Single Malt Ceramic OB, 50%, 75cl
ROSEBANK 12 years – Flora and Fauna, 43%, 70cl

SPRINGBANK | 1885 | Scotland/Écosse | Campbeltown | Hazelburn, Longrow, Springbank

Located out in the wildness of the Mull of Kintyre—immortalized by Paul McCartney—this distillery, the property of the Mitchell family, produces one of the richest single malts ever conceived. Characterized by creamy beeswax and exotic fruit notes, the 12- and 21-year-old versions have made an impression on generations of connoisseurs. The much-prized Local Barley of the 1960s, with telltale notes of leather and pipe tobacco, also bear investigation. And, as if that were not enough, Springbank distills a peaty single malt called Longrow that can compete with the best Islay.

Située dans le très sauvage Mull of Kintyre, immortalisé par Paul McCartney, cette distillerie, propriété de la famille Mitchell, élabore l'un des single malts les plus riches jamais produits à ce jour. Marquées par des notes crémeuses de cire d'abeille et de fruits exotiques, les versions de 12 et 21 ans ont marqué des générations d'amateurs. Les très prisés Local Barley des années 1960 aux notes caractéristiques de cuir et de tabac à pipe ne sont pas en reste. Et comme si cela ne suffisait pas, Springbank distille un single malt tourbé baptisé Longrow qui rivalise avec les meilleurs Islay.

Great whiskies | Les grands whiskies
SPRINGBANK 1966 OB, 60.7%, 75cl
SPRINGBANK 27 years 1969 Dumpy – Signatory Vintage, 51.8%, 70cl
SPRINGBANK 34 years 1970 Prestonfield – Signatory Vintage, 51.2%, 70cl
LONGROW 1973 OB, 46%, 75cl
SPRINGBANK 21 years 1974 Parchment Label OB, 46%, 75cl
SPRINGBANK 50 years Millenium OB, 40.5%, 70cl
SPRINGBANK 40 years Millenium OB, 40.1%, 70cl
SPRINGBANK 25 years Dumpy OB, 46%, 70cl
LONGROW 25 years OB, 46%, 70cl
SPRINGBANK 12 years – Samaroli, 57.1%, 75cl

The classic | Le classique
SPRINGBANK 18 years OB, 46%, 70cl

STRATHISLA | 1786 | Scotland/Écosse | Speyside | Strathisla

With its water wheel and its two pagodas, Strathisla, often presented as the home of Chivas, is one of the chief attractions of the region. Behind its picturesque setting, however, there lurks an immense whisky. Like other Speysides, this delicate single malt expresses its potential as it ages. Versions from the 1960s and 1970s by independent bottlers Gordon & MacPhail—in particular certain refill sherry casks—have developed into something richly mellow. Rarer still, a Strathisla from the late 1930s provides one of the great moments of tasting.

Avec sa roue à aubes et ses deux pagodes, Strathisla, souvent présentée comme la maison de Chivas, est l'une des attractions de la région. Mais au-delà de son caractère pittoresque se cache un immense whisky. Comme d'autres Speyside, ce single malt délicat exprime tout son potentiel en vieillissant. Les millésimes des années 1960/70 de l'embouteilleur indépendant Gordon & MacPhail, notamment certains fûts de sherry de second remplissage, se révèlent particulièrement onctueux. Encore plus rares, les Strathisla de la fin des années 1930 vous feront vivre de grands moments de dégustation.

Great whiskies | Les grands whiskies
STRATHISLA 1937 – Gordon & MacPhail, 40%, 75cl
STRATHISLA 34 years 1937 Connoisseurs Choice – Gordon & MacPhail, 43%, 75cl
STRATHISLA 1960 Rare Vintage – Gordon & MacPhail, 50%, 70cl
STRATHISLA 1965 – Gordon & MacPhail, 48%, 70cl
STRATHISLA 1967 Single Cask – Gordon & MacPhail, 50%, 70cl
STRATHISLA 31 years 1968 Millenium Edition – Signatory Vintage, 53.2%, 70cl
STRATHISLA 16 years 1973 Rare Vintage – Gordon & MacPhail, 62.3%, 75cl
STRATHISLA 35 years Bicentenary OB, 46%, 70cl
STRATHISLA 30 years – Gordon & MacPhail, 46%, 70cl
STRATHISLA 10 years, Rotation early 1960s OB, 43%, 75cl

The classic | Le classique
STRATHISLA 12 years OB, 40%, 70cl

TALISKER | 1830 | Scotland/Écosse | Isle of Skye | Talisker

Talisker produces a single malt of inimitable style, marked by spicy, iodine, and medicinal notes. Revealed to the general public in 1988 in the Classic Malts range, it had already enjoyed a steady reputation among a number of those in the know. Inaccessible and too austere for certain palates, like other very great single malts, it presents as well at 8 as at 30 years, revealing notes of bitter orange and cool tobacco on aging. Some rare sherry-cask versions from the 1950s reveal sweet and savory notes oscillating between red fruit and licorice.

Talisker élabore un single malt au style inimitable, marqué par des notes épicées, iodées et médicinales. Révélé au grand public en 1988 par la gamme des Classic Malts, il jouissait jusque-là d'une solide réputation auprès de quelques amateurs avertis. Inaccessible et trop austère pour certains palais, comme d'autres très grands single malts, il se révèle aussi bien à 8 ans qu'à 30 ans, le vieillissement révélant des notes d'orange amère et de tabac froid. Quelques rares versions sherry cask des années 1950 dévoilent des notes sucrées salées oscillant entre les fruits rouges et la réglisse.

Great whiskies | Les grands whiskies
TALISKER 21 years 1952 Black Label Connoisseurs Choice – Gordon & MacPhail, 43%, 75cl
SECRET STILLS 50 years 1955 Number One – Gordon & MacPhail, 45%, 70cl
TALISKER 1957 – Gordon & MacPhail, 53.5%, 75cl
TALISKER 34 years 1977 Limited Edition OB, 54.6%, 70cl
TALISKER 20 years 1981 OB, 62%, 70cl
TALISKER 25 years 1982 Limited Edition OB, 58.1%, 70cl
TALISKER 20 years 1982 Limited Edition OB, 58.8%, 70cl
TALISKER 30 years OB, 49.5%, 70cl
TALISKER 12 years, Rotation 1970s OB, 43%, 75cl
TALISKER Limited Edition OB, 60%, 70cl

The classic | Le classique
TALISKER 18 years OB, 45.8%, 70cl

TOBERMORY | 1798 | Scotland/Écosse | Isle of Mull | Ledaig, Tobermory

The only distillery on the Isle of Mull, Tobermory distills two single malts: the eponymous unpeated version and a very peaty expression christened Ledaig. After remaining inactive for more than forty years, Tobermory reopened in 1972 under the name Ledaig. Until its closure in 1975 due to bankruptcy, Ledaig/Tobermory produced several exceptional versions marketed by independent bottlers. Tobermory resumed activity in 1993. Riding the wave of the passion for peaty whisky, Ledaig is becoming increasingly popular. Certain sherry-cask versions can recall a great Ledaig of the 1970s.

Unique distillerie de l'île de Mull, Tobermory élabore deux single malts : une version non tourbée éponyme et une version très tourbée baptisée Ledaig. Après plus de 40 ans de fermeture, Tobermory fut relancée en 1972 sous le nom de Ledaig. Jusqu'à sa fermeture en 1975 pour cause de faillite Ledaig/Tobermory donna naissance à plusieurs versions d'exception, commercialisées par des embouteilleurs indépendants. Profitant de l'engouement pour les whiskies tourbés, Ledaig est de plus en plus populaire. Certaines versions sherry cask ne sont pas sans rappeler les grands Ledaig des années 1970.

Great whiskies | Les grands whiskies
LEDAIG 1972 OB, 51.9%, 70cl
LEDAIG 1972 Connoisseurs Choice – Gordon & MacPhail, 40%, 75cl
TOBERMORY 32 years 1972 Green Label OB, 50.1%, 70cl
TOBERMORY 32 years 1972 Red Label OB, 49.5%, 70cl
TOBERMORY 33 years 1972 Moon Import OB, 49%, 70cl
TOBERMORY 1972 Connoisseurs Choice Gradient Brown Label for Meregalli Import – Gordon & MacPhail, 40%, 75cl
TOBERMORY 6 years 1972 Connoisseurs Choice Black Label for Giacone Import – Gordon & MacPhail, 40%, 75cl
LEDAIG 1974 OB, 43%, 70cl
LEDAIG 30 years 1974 Cask Strength Collection – Signatory Vintage, 48.7%, 70cl
LEDAIG 2004 Artist Aged 10 Years – LMDW, 60.4%, 70cl

The classic | Le classique
LEDAIG 10 years Un-chillfiltered OB, 46.3%, 70cl

YAMAZAKI | 1923 | Japan/Japon | Osaka prefecture | Yamazaki

In 2014, a sherry-cask Yamazaki was voted the best single malt in the world by whisky expert Jim Murray. In point of fact, this consecration does little more than to confirm what many a connoisseur had suspected for years: the exceptional quality of the oldest Japanese single malt. Certain collectors are willing to spend more than $115,000 USD/£90,000 GBP for a bottle of its 50 year old. A victim of its global success, Yamazaki has been running sub quota for a number of years. It is, however, still feasible to find a bottle of 18 year old, which is quite simply one of the best sherry-cask whiskies in the world.

En 2014, un Yamazaki sherry cask est élu meilleur single malt au monde par l'expert Jim Murray. En réalité, cette consécration ne fait que confirmer ce que bon nombre d'amateurs savent déjà depuis quelques années : la qualité exceptionnelle du plus vieux single malt japonais. Certains collectionneurs sont même prêts à dépenser plus de 100 000 € pour une bouteille de 50 ans. Victime de son succès planétaire, Yamazaki est sous contingent depuis quelques années. Cependant il est encore possible de se procurer une bouteille de 18 ans, tout simplement l'un des meilleurs sherry casks au monde.

Great whiskies | Les grands whiskies
YAMAZAKI 1980 Vintage Malt OB, 56%, 70cl
YAMAZAKI 1984 OB, 48%, 70cl
YAMAZAKI 30 years 1986 The Owner's Cask OB, 60%, 70cl
YAMAZAKI 1990 Vintage Malt OB, 61%, 70cl
YAMAZAKI 1993 Single Cask OB, 57.5%, 70cl
YAMAZAKI 1995 The Owner's Cask OB, 54.9%, 70cl
YAMAZAKI Tokyo Int. Barshow 2013 Mizunara OB, 50%, 70cl
YAMAZAKI Sherry Cask Edition 2016 OB, 48%, 70cl
YAMAZAKI 25 years OB, 43%, 70cl
YAMAZAKI Mizunara OB, 48%, 70cl

The classic | Le classique
YAMAZAKI 18 years OB, 43%, 70cl

YOICHI | 1934 | Japan/Japon | Hokkaïdo prefecture | Yoichi

Twice voted best single malt in the world by *Whisky Magazine*, in 2002 and 2008, this single malt, inextricably linked to the founding father of Japanese whisky, Masataka Taketsuru, is available in every style, peaty or unpeated, and after every type of aging, from new oak barrels to first-fill sherry casks. Whatever the case, the same magic is at work, resulting in a spicy style and with notes of leather that emerge beyond the peat, vanilla, and sherry. Although the older and vintage versions have vanished from the market temporarily, it is still possible to taste them in a few specialized bars.

Élu à deux reprises meilleur single malt au monde, en 2002 et 2008 par la revue *Whisky Magazine*, ce single malt, intimement lié au père fondateur du whisky japonais Masataka Taketsuru, décline tous les styles, tourbé ou non tourbé, et tous les vieillissements, du fût de chêne neuf au fût de sherry de premier remplissage. Et à chaque fois, la magie opère, le style épicé et les notes de cuir émergeant au-delà de la tourbe, de la vanille et du sherry. Si les versions âgées et millésimées ont provisoirement disparu du marché, il est encore possible de les déguster dans quelques bars spécialisés.

Great whiskies | Les grands whiskies
YOICHI 1987 Single Cask OB, 55%, 70cl
YOICHI 17 years 1987 Peaty OB, 53.5%, 70cl
YOICHI 1988 Heavily Peated Single Cask OB, 62%, 70cl
YOICHI 1989 Single Cask OB, 60%, 70cl
YOICHI 1989 Whisky Live Tokyo 2010 OB, 62%, 70cl
YOICHI 1991 Single Cask OB, 62%, 70cl
YOICHI 1991 Heavily Peated Single Cask OB, 62%, 70cl
YOICHI 20 years OB, 52%, 70cl
YOICHI 10 years OB, 62.2%, 70cl
YOICHI 15 years OB, 60.4%, 75cl

The classic | Le classique
YOICHI Single Malt OB, 45%, 70cl

AMERICAN WHISKEY

What nation in the world can compete with Scotland, the homeland of single malt? Ireland? Japan, perhaps? Admittedly, these countries have the wind in their sails, and never before have so many Irish or Japanese distilleries been established and so much whisky exported. And yet, apart from two or three heavyweight producers, the majority tend to be small businesses.

Another country, however, working in a very different style of whisky, has emerged as a potential contender: the United States. And one region in particular: Kentucky. This state is, for American whiskey, what Speyside is for single malt scotch. One needs only to visit the bars and restaurants of New York or any other major American city to witness the scale of the phenomenon.

American whiskey—especially Kentucky bourbon and rye, but also Tennessee whiskey—is now found everywhere, and not just in cocktail bars. The dynamism of American distilleries has given rise to quality American products of great aromatic complexity.

It all began at the beginning of the 1980s with the advent of the first single-barrel bourbons. Buffalo Trace distillery blazed the trail and was soon followed by Jim Beam, Four Roses, Maker's Mark, and Woodford Reserve. The most recent distillery to date, Michter's, offers magnificent versions that have breathed new life into the genre.

Collectors, too, are seeing the light: while the popularity of Scottish single malt and Japanese whisky—albeit increasingly scarce—remains at its peak, that of old Kentucky whiskeys is certainly growing steadily.

———

Quelle autre région du monde peut rivaliser avec l'Écosse, pays du single malt ? L'Irlande, le Japon... Certes ces pays ont le vent en poupe et il ne s'est jamais autant créé de distilleries et exporté d'Irish ou de Japanese whisky qu'en ce moment, mais en dehors de deux ou trois grands producteurs on ne trouve que de petites distilleries en devenir.

Une autre nation, qui élabore un style de whisky très différent, est un rival en puissance : les États-Unis et en particulier une région, le Kentucky. Cet État est à l'American whiskey ce que le Speyside est au single malt écossais. Il suffit de se rendre aux Etats-Unis dans les bars et les restaurants de New York ou d'autres grandes villes américaines pour prendre la mesure de ce phénomène.

L'American whiskey, notamment le bourbon et le rye du Kentucky, sans oublier le Tennessee whiskey, n'ont pas envahi que les bars à cocktails. Le dynamisme des distilleries américaines a donné naissance à des whiskeys américains de dégustation d'une grande complexité aromatique.

Tout a démarré au début des années 1980 avec l'avènement des premiers single barrels bourbons. La distillerie Buffalo Trace fut pionnière en la matière, imitée par Jim Beam, Four Roses, Maker's Mark ou encore Woodford Reserve. La dernière distillerie en date, Michter's, propose également des versions très qualitatives qui renouvellent le genre.

D'ailleurs, les collectionneurs ne s'y trompent pas : si la cote du single malt écossais et du whisky japonais, victime de sa raréfaction, est toujours au sommet, celle des vieux whiskeys du Kentucky ne cesse de grimper.

Great whiskies | Les grands whiskies
PAPPY VAN WINKLE'S 23 years Family Reserve OB, 47.8%, 75cl
PAPPY VAN WINKLE'S 20 years Family Reserve OB, 45.2%, 70cl
VAN WINKLE 13 years Family Reserve OB, 47.8%, 70cl
SAZERAC RYE 18 years 1984 OB, 45%, 75cl
GEORGE T. STAGG OB, 71.35%, 75cl

The classics | Les classiques
ELIJAH CRAIG 12 years Barrel Proof OB, 67.8%, 70cl
BLANTON'S Original OB, 46.5%, 70cl
BOOKER'S OB, 63.7%, 70cl
MICHTER'S US 1 Bourbon OB, 45.7%, 70cl
W. L.WELLER 12 years OB, 45%, 75cl

BLENDS

By the beginning of the 2000s, blends, paling in comparison with single malts, had fallen out of fashion. In Europe, people watched as, overnight, many historic brands went under, and interest in the category was, going forward, confined to the ongoing global commercial spat between Johnnie Walker and Chivas.

Since then, though, a number of bold visionaries have picked up the baton, and a new nation has arrived on the international stage: Japan. Though Japanese whisky first made headlines when one earned the title of best single malt in the world in 2001, it is above all the country's blends that make its name beyond its borders. Today, more than 80% of Japanese whiskies sold throughout the world are blends.

Although the Japanese have kept faith with Scottish methods of production, they have borrowed the art of blending from France. The end result presents a balance and smoothness that contrasts boldly with the dryness of some Scottish blends. Thus, over the last ten years, Japanese blends and blended malts have taken all the prizes at international competitions.

Sales, too, are on the up. In Scotland, the homeland of blending, new master blenders are launching craft vintages in which each ingredient is carefully monitored. John Glaser, founder of Compass Box, is the pioneer of this movement, which is only just getting off the ground.

A telltale sign of the revival of this category—unlike the blends of yesteryear, which are often older and contain a high proportion of single malt—collectors have begun to show an interest in recent limited series.

———

Au début des années 2000, le blend était passé de mode, le single malt ayant seul droit de cité. Sur le vieux continent, on assiste du jour au lendemain à la disparition de nombreuses marques historiques et l'intérêt de la catégorie se résume désormais à une guerre commerciale planétaire entre Johnnie Walker et Chivas. C'était sans compter sur l'audace de quelques visionnaires et surtout l'avènement d'une nouvelle nation sur la scène internationale : le Japon.

Même si en 2001 le whisky japonais fit jaser en remportant le titre de meilleur single malt au monde, ce sont en réalité les blends qui lui permettent d'exister en dehors de ses frontières. Aujourd'hui, plus de 80% des whiskies japonais vendus dans le monde sont des blends. Si les japonais sont fidèles aux méthodes de production écossaises, ils ont emprunté à la France l'art de l'assemblage. Au final, l'équilibre et la douceur dont ils font preuve contrastent avec la sécheresse de certains blends écossais. Ainsi, depuis une dizaine d'années, blends et blended malts japonais trustent toutes les récompenses dans les compétitions internationales. Et leurs ventes ne cessent de progresser.

En Écosse, la patrie originelle du blend, des nouveaux Master Blenders se lancent dans la production de cuvées artisanales où chaque ingrédient est soigneusement monitoré. John Glaser, fondateur de Compass Box, est le pionnier de ce mouvement qui n'en est qu'à ses balbutiements.

Signe du renouveau de la catégorie, au-delà des blends d'antan souvent plus âgés et à forte proportion de single malt, certaines séries limitées récentes commencent à intéresser les collectionneurs.

Great whiskies | Les grands whiskies
JOHNNIE WALKER 200th Anniversary OB, 46.3%, 75cl
CHIVAS 50 years Royal Salute OB, 40%, 70cl
BALLANTINE'S 40 years OB, 43%, 70cl
NIKKA 40 years The Nikka OB, 43%, 70cl
SUNTORY 30 years Hibiki OB, 43%, 70cl

The classics | Les classiques
NIKKA 21 years Taketsuru OB, 43%, 70cl
BIG PEAT Remarkable Regional Malts – D. Laing, 46%, 70cl
CHIVAS 25 years Regal OB, 40%, 70cl
GREAT KING STREET Artist's Blend – Compass Box, 43%, 70cl
NIKKA From the Barrel OB, 51%, 50cl

NEW WORLD WHISKIES | LES WHISKIES DU NOUVEAU MONDE

Since the early 2000s, the world of whisky has been gripped by a transformation that has shaken up the hegemony of scotch, which has lasted more than a century. In the wake of Japan—the most recent nation to gain universal acclaim—hundreds of malt distilleries have begun to bloom all over the world. Lovers of Scottish single malt observe this phenomenon with a mix of interest and unease. Developments over the last ten years, however, have surely convinced them that they will have to keep an eye on these new arrivals in the future.

Above and beyond the many gold medals garnered by certain avant-garde distilleries, these whiskies impose an idiosyncratic style that is often linked to their geographical location. With Amrut in India and Kavalan in Taiwan, the tropical climate in which the barrels age produces young whiskies of astonishing maturity. In Sweden, but also in France, distilleries are increasingly sourcing their oak locally rather than resorting to bourbon barrels or sherry casks, as is the custom. This aging policy has resulted in single malts boasting hitherto unprecedented specifities. While this transcontinental class is being spearheaded by distilleries such as Kavalan, Amrut, Penderyn in Wales, Mackmyra in Sweden, Warenghem in France, and Hellyers Road in Tasmania, other countries and producers are already making waves.

———

Le monde du whisky est en pleine ébullition depuis le début des années 2000, bousculant l'hégémonie plus que centenaire du scotch whisky. Dans la foulée du Japon, dernière nation historique reconnue mondialement, des centaines de distilleries de malt sont en train d'émerger aux quatre coins de la planète. Les amateurs de single malts écossais regardent ce phénomène avec un mélange d'intérêt et de méfiance. L'évolution de ces dix dernières années devrait pourtant les convaincre qu'il faudra compter avec ces pays à l'avenir.

Au-delà des nombreuses médailles d'or remportées par certaines distilleries avant-gardistes, ces whiskies imposent un style unique souvent lié à leur situation géographique. Chez Amrut en Inde et Kavalan à Taiwan, les fûts vieillissent en climat tropical, donnant naissance à de jeunes whiskies d'une maturité surprenante. En Suède, mais aussi en France, les distilleries s'appuient de plus en plus sur les ressources en chêne local plutôt que sur les habituels fûts de bourbon ou de sherry. Une maîtrise du vieillissement qui se traduit par des single malts aux typicités inconnues jusqu'alors. Même si des distilleries comme Kavalan, Amrut, Penderyn au Pays de Galles, Mackmyra en Suède, Warenghem en France ou Hellyers Road en Tasmanie sont les actuels porte-drapeaux de cette catégorie transcontinentale, d'autres pays et d'autres acteurs sont déjà en train d'émerger.

The classics | Les classiques
ARMORIK Maitre de Chai OB, 46%, 70cl
BOX WHISKY Dalvve OB, 46%, 70cl
EDDU Silver OB, 40%, 70cl
HELLYERS ROAD 10 years OB, 46.2%, 70cl
MACKMYRA Ten Years OB, 46.1%, 70cl
PENDERYN Madeira OB, 46%, 70cl
THE ENGLISH WHISKY CO. Smokey OB, 43%, 70cl
NANTOU Omar Single Malt OB, 46%, 70cl
PAUL JOHN Edited OB, 46%, 70cl
GLAN AR MOR Kornog OB, 46%, 70cl

GRAIN WHISKIES | WHISKY DE GRAIN

Grain whisky, an essential ingredient in blend production, is seldom consumed out of the barrel. In the 1990s, a few Scottish producers carried out marketing tests, with no real success. The current rarity of older single malts has recently pushed some independent bottlers to release grain whiskies from the 1960s and 1970s, which have delicious vanilla, caramel, and coconut notes. However, Japan has rebuilt its reputation. The Nikka Whisky group is alone in producing a grain whisky from corn rather than wheat, distilled in a traditional Coffey type still. Richer and more complex, it is reminiscent of certain Kentucky bourbons.

———

Ingrédient indispensable à la production de blends, le whisky de grain est rarement consommé tel quel. Dans les années 1990, des producteurs écossais avaient fait des essais de commercialisation mais sans réel succès. La raréfaction actuelle des vieux single malts a poussé quelques embouteilleurs indépendants à proposer des whiskies de grains des années 1960/70, qui se distinguent par des notes gourmandes de vanille, de caramel et de noix de coco. Mais une fois encore, c'est le Japon qui lui a redonné ses lettres de noblesse. Le groupe Nikka Whisky est ainsi le seul à produire un whisky de grain à base de maïs plutôt que de blé, distillé dans un alambic traditionnel de type Coffey. Plus riche et plus complexe, ce dernier n'est pas sans rappeler certains bourbons du Kentucky.

Great whiskies | Les grands whiskies
DUMBARTON 25 years 1959 – Cadenhead, 46%, 75cl
NORTH BRITISH 45 years 1962 Prestonfield – Signatory Vintage, 59.9%, 70cl
CAMBUS GRAIN 31 years 1964 – Signatory Vintage, 43.8%, 70cl
CARSEBRIDGE 40 years 1965 – Berry Bros, 46%, 70cl
KAWASAKI 1976 – Ichiro's Choice OB, 65.6%, 70cl
CAMERONBRIDGE 39 years 1976 Hogshead Cask Strength Collection – Signatory Vintage, 49.8%, 70cl
CALEDONIAN GRAIN 23 years 1976 – Signatory Vintage, 58.5%, 70cl
INVERGORDON 22 years OB, 45%, 70cl

The classics | Les classiques
HEDONISM – Compass Box, 46%, 70cl
NIKKA Coffey Grain OB, 45%, 70cl

MICRO- & CRAFT DISTILLERIES

The micro-distillery phenomenon arose in the US in the 1980s. Today, there are almost a thousand accross the US, and the majority are craft distilleries, which control the entire chain of production, even to the point of growing their own grains. Although most produce every type of spirit, their main effect has been to revive an appreciation for a style that had long fallen out of favor: rye whiskey. In recent years, other distilleries following this model have been launched throughout the world (especially in Australia, Canada, and Europe), and in agricultural and urban areas. Often aged in small casks, which are easier to store and accelerate an aging process that brings out the woody notes, these craft spirits will need time to show their full potential.

———

Né aux Etats-Unis dans les années 1980, le phénomène des micro-distilleries touche désormais tous les états et la plupart des grandes villes américaines. On en compterait près d'un millier, dont une majorité de crafts, maîtrisant toute la chaîne de production, allant même jusqu'à cultiver leurs céréales. Si la plupart d'entre elles produisent tous types de spiritueux, elles ont surtout remis au goût du jour un style tombé en désuétude : le rye whiskey. Sur ce modèle, d'autres distilleries à travers le monde se sont récemment lancées. Souvent vieillis en petites barriques, plus faciles à stocker et qui accélèrent le vieillissement au profit des notes boisées, ces craft spirits auront besoin de temps pour démontrer leur potentiel.

The classics | Les classiques
DAD'S HAT Pennsylvania Rye Port Wine Finish OB, 47%, 70cl
DOMAINE DES HAUTES GLACES Les Moissons – Single Malt Organic OB, 44%, 70cl
FEW Rye Whiskey OB, 46.5%, 70cl
HUDSON Baby Bourbon OB, 46%, 35cl
KOVAL Single Barrel Millet OB, 40%, 50cl
MCCARTHY'S Oregon Single Malt OB, 42.5%, 70cl
NY DISTILLING CO. 3 years Ragtime Rye Whiskey OB, 45.2%, 70cl
SONOMA 2nd Chance Wheat OB, 49%, 70cl
WESTLAND American Single Malt Peated OB, 46%, 70cl
WIDOW JANE Rye Mash OB, 45.5%, 70cl

Appendix

Annexe

Glossary

AGE: In both Scotland and Ireland, the minimum age of a whisky is three years. For a blend, the age printed on the label is that of the youngest whisky in the bottle. A whisky ceases to mature once bottled.

ANGELS' SHARE: The natural evaporation of alcohol through the cask while the whisky is aging. This evaporation is estimated at 2%–4% per annum.

BLENDED SCOTCH: A whisky produced from a mixture of grain and malt whisky selected from several Scottish grain and malt distilleries.

BOOTLEGGER: In 1862, Abraham Lincoln took the decision to reintroduce taxes on whiskey in order to fund the Union's war effort. The conflict thus witnessed the emergence of "bootleggers," who sold smuggled whiskey, hidden in the leggings of their boots, to Union and Confederate soldiers alike.

BOURBON: An American whiskey originally produced in Kentucky that is made from a minimum of 51% corn and aged in new American oak.

BOURBON BARREL: An oak barrel of a capacity of 53 US gallons (200 liters). Built from staves of American white oak and previously used for aging bourbon, it is then used to make whiskies.

CASK STRENGTH: Whisky bottled natural proof straight from the barrel, undiluted. It can reach more than 60% alcohol by volume (ABV).

CASK/BARREL/BUTT: Terms designating oak barrels of various types.

CHILL FILTRATION: The temperature of the whisky is reduced to 32°F–36°F (0°C–2°C) in order to extract the maximum of fatty acids that cause the cloudy appearance of some whiskies with a degree of alcohol lower than 46% by volume.

DRAM: Scottish word meaning a measure of alcohol. Now part of everyday speech, it is employed especially to designate a glass of whisky (in particular as ordered in a pub): the famous "wee dram" thus means a small glass of whisky.

EXTRA-AGING: A period of aging that can vary from anything between three and twenty-four months, further refining the character of the whisky. "Extra-aging," or finishing, occurs at the end of a period of aging of several years in casks that once contained wine, port, sherry, or Madeira. The technique is designed to broaden the range of the whisky's flavors.

FINISH: The flavors and aromas of a whisky that remain perceptible after swallowing the mouthful. It is measured by its length: a long finish is usually considered superior.

FINISHING: After aging in the traditional fashion, a whisky is "finished" by being transferred into a cask from a different source and with different characteristics, in which it continues aging.

FIRST FILL: A cask that, having been employed to age bourbon or sherry, is then used for maturing a Scotch whisky for the first time.

GRAIN WHISKY: A whisky made from corn or wheat, continuously distilled in a column still and aged for a minimum of three years in oak casks.

HOGSHEAD: In whisky-making, a cask with a capacity of around 66 US gallons (250 liters), rebuilt out of staves from bourbon barrels or other pre-used staves.

INDEPENDENT BOTTLING: Bottling carried out by a private company that purchases batches of casks from whisky producers. Bottling is often carried out thematically, cask by cask: single cask, cask strength, un-chillfiltered, etc. The visual identity of the range promotes the bottler and its distinctive features, and only then the distillery.

IRISH WHISKEY: A whiskey made from fermented grain must (malted or unmalted), generally distilled three times and aged for a minimum three years in oak casks in Ireland. The minimum degree of alcohol for an Irish whiskey is 40% by volume.

MALT WHISKY: Whisky made from 100% of the same malted grain (barley in Scotland), distilled in copper pot stills and aged for a minimum period of three years in oak casks.

NOSE: The set of olfactory aromas of a whisky. The primary organ in tasting, the nose is deployed throughout: from the first nose before the whisky is even opened to the empty glass, which can reveal new notes.

OFFICIAL BOTTLING (OB): Bottling undertaken on the initiative of the distillery owner. Such bottlings are characterized by a very strong visual identity conveyed by a label and a bottle especially designed for the brand, as well as by the extent of the range offered: examples include Glenmorangie Original, Extra Matured, Extremely Rare, and The Quarter Century.

PEAT: Natural fuel resulting from the partial decomposition of vegetal matter, which is cut and dried into briquettes that are used for drying the malted barley used in the production of smoky whiskies on the isles of Islay and Skye, among others.

PHENOLS: Chemical compounds added to the whisky by the smoke from a peat fire. Phenols bestow smoky flavors and aromas on the alcohol.

PURE POT STILL: Composed of a 50/50 mixture of malted and unmalted barley and then distilled three times in pot stills, pure pot still is the traditional Irish whiskey. Its origins date back to the beginning of the eighteenth century, when it was produced from a mixture of grains, primarily malted and unmalted barley, though it might also contain a certain percentage of wheat, oats, and rye. At that time, it acted as a subterfuge for reducing the tax on whiskey by circumventing the duty on malt. Today, this style of whiskey is produced at the Midleton distillery in the south of Ireland.

QUAICH: A traditional drinking cup with two handles in which whisky is served, in particular when welcoming a guest. Today generally made of tin or stainless steel, it can be compared with the *tastevin*, a shallow cup used in France for tasting wines.

REFILL: In Scotland and Ireland, this designates a cask that has been used at least once to age a whisky (the opposite of a first fill).

SCOTCH WHISKY: A whisky produced, aged, and bottled in Scotland, made from grains, distilled in stills, and aged in oak casks for a minimum period of three years. The minimum degree of alcohol for a Scotch is 40% volume (80° proof).

SHERRY BUTT: An oak cask with a capacity varying from about 130 to 185 US gallons (500 to 700 liters) and used for aging the wines of Jerez de la Frontera and sherry generally. Varieties of sherry include Fino, Manzanilla, Amontillado, Oloroso, and Pedro Ximénez. The sherry butts most sought-after by distilleries are those that contained Oloroso and Pedro Ximénez.

SINGLE CASK: The bottling of a whisky from a single cask or barrel.

SINGLE MALT: Malt whisky originating in one and only one distillery.

SMALL BATCH: Blend of several whiskies from a relatively small number of select casks.

STILL: A kind of copper kettle designed to separate and bring out certain elements from the product by heating and then cooling it. Stills were employed by the Arabs in the tenth century to produce essences and perfumes and were subsequently introduced into Scotland for distilling alcohol.

UN-CHILLFILTERED: Whiskies not filtered by chilling, in order to preserve the maximum of fatty acids to create a soft, silky texture. These whiskies generally present a degree of alcohol equal to or higher than 46% by volume.

VATTED/BLENDED MALT: Single malts selected from various malt distilleries and subsequently blended.

WHISKEY/WHISKY: The difference in spelling is primarily geographic: "whiskey" is commonly used in the United States and Ireland, "whisky" is usually used in the rest of the world. This grain alcohol contains at least 40% alcohol by volume and is aged in oak casks.

Glossaire

ÂGE : l'âge minimum d'un whisky est de 3 ans en Écosse et en Irlande. L'âge apparaissant sur l'étiquette est celui du whisky le plus jeune contenu dans la bouteille s'il y a assemblage. Une fois embouteillé, un whisky ne vieillit plus.

AFFINAGE : après vieillissement de façon traditionnel, le whisky est affiné lorsqu'il est transféré dans un fût d'origine et de caractéristiques différents pour y bénéficier d'un vieillissement prolongé.

ALAMBIC : sorte de bouilloire en cuivre destinée à séparer et magnifier certains éléments d'un même produit, par chauffage puis refroidissement. L'alambic fut utilisé par les Arabes au xe siècle afin de produire des essences et des parfums. Plus tard, il fut introduit en Écosse pour la distillation de l'alcool.

ANGELS' SHARE : « la part des anges ». Évaporation naturelle de l'alcool à travers le fût au cours de l'élevage du whisky. Cette évaporation est estimée à 2 % par an en Écosse.

BLENDED SCOTCH : whisky élaboré à partir d'un mélange de whisky de grain et de whisky de malt, sélectionnés au sein de plusieurs distilleries de grain et de malt écossaises.

BOOTLEGGER : en 1862 Abraham Lincoln prit la décision de réintroduire les taxes sur le whiskey afin de financer l'effort de guerre des États de l'Union. C'est durant cette guerre que l'on vit apparaître les bootleggers qui vendaient du whiskey de contrebande dissimulé dans les jambières (*legger*) de leurs bottes (*boot*) aux soldats nordistes et sudistes.

BOURBON BARREL : fût de chêne d'une capacité d'environ 180 à 200 litres. Construit à partir de douelles de chêne blanc américain, utilisé préalablement pour l'élevage du bourbon puis pour celui des scotch whiskies.

BOURBON : whiskey américain produit entre autre dans le Kentucky, élaboré à partir d'un minimum de 51 % de maïs, puis élevé en fût de chêne neuf américains.

CASK/BARREL/BUTT : termes désignant un fût de chêne.

CASK STRENGTH : « brut de fût ». Whisky mis en bouteilles à son degré naturel, sans ajout d'eau. Le degré peut atteindre plus de 60 % vol.

CHILL FILTRATION : « filtration à froid ». La température d'un whisky est ramenée à 0 °C -2 °C, afin d'en extraire le maximum d'acides gras à l'origine de l'aspect trouble des whiskies présentant un degré d'alcool inférieur à 46 % vol.

DRAM : mot écossais désignant une mesure d'alcool. Passé dans le langage courant, il est employé surtout pour désigner un verre de whisky (notamment lors d'une commande au pub), « *wee dram* » indique ainsi un petit verre de whisky.

EXTRA-MATURATION : période d'élevage pouvant varier de 3 à 24 mois en général, permettant d'affiner le caractère d'un whisky. L'« extra-maturation », ou affinage, est pratiquée au terme d'une période de maturation de plusieurs années dans des fûts ayant contenu du vin, du porto, du sherry ou du madère. Cette technique vise à étendre la palette aromatique des whiskies.

FINALE : les arômes et saveurs d'un whisky subsistant en bouche après la gorgée avalée. Elle est mesurée par sa longueur : une finale longue est habituellement perçue comme meilleure.

FIRST FILL : « premier remplissage ». Fût qui, après avoir été utilisé pour l'élevage du bourbon ou du sherry, est utilisé pour la première fois pour le vieillissement d'un scotch whisky.

GRAIN WHISKY : whisky élaboré à partir de maïs ou de blé, distillé en continu dans un alambic à colonnes, élevé pour un minimum de trois ans en fût de chêne.

HOGSHEAD : fût d'une capacité d'environ 250 litres, reconstitué à partir de douelles d'ex-fûts de bourbon et de douelles usagées.

INDEPENDENT BOTTLING : « embouteillage indépendant » ou de négoce. Ces embouteillages sont réalisés à l'initiative d'une société privée qui achète en lot des fûts auprès des producteurs de whisky. Les mises en bouteilles sont souvent faites au fût par fût autour d'une thématique : single casks, cask stength, un-chillfiltered. L'identité visuelle de la gamme met en avant l'embouteilleur et sa spécificité, puis la distillerie.

IRISH WHISKEY : whiskey élaboré a partir d'un moût fermenté de céréales (maltées ou non maltées), distillé

le plus souvent trois fois et vieilli pour un minimum de trois ans en fût de chêne en Irlande. Le degré minimum pour un irish whiskey est de 40 % vol.

MALT WHISKY : whisky élaboré à partir de 100 % d'une même céréale maltée (l'orge pour l'Écosse), distillé dans des alambics en cuivre à pot et élevé pour une période de trois ans minimum en fûts de chêne.

NEZ : ensemble des arômes olfactifs d'un whisky. Organe central de la dégustation, le nez est sollicité tout au long de celle-ci : du premier nez, avant que le whisky ne se soit ouvert, au verre vide qui dévoile de nouvelles notes.

OFFICIAL BOTTLING : « embouteillage officiel ». Il s'agit de mises en bouteilles faites à l'initiative de propriétaires de distilleries. Ces embouteillages se caractérisent par une identité visuelle très forte véhiculée par une étiquette et un flacon spécialement conçus pour la marque, mais aussi par l'étendue de la gamme proposée : Glenmorangie Original, Extra Matured, Extremely Rare, The Quarter Century.

PEAT : « tourbe ». Combustible utilisé pour le séchage de l'orge maltée destinée à la production des whiskies fumés des îles d'Islay et de Skye entre autres.

PHÉNOLS : composés chimiques cédés au whisky par la fumée d'un feu de tourbe. Les phénols apportent à l'alcool des arômes et des saveurs fumés.

PURE POT STILL : élaboré à partir d'un mélange à 50/50 d'orge maltée et non maltée puis distillé trois fois dans des alambics pot still, le pure pot still est l'Irish whiskey traditionnel. Ses origines remontent au début du XVIIIe siècle. Il était alors produit à partir d'un mélange de céréales, essentiellement de l'orge maltée et non maltée, mais il pouvait également contenir un certain pourcentage de blé, d'avoine et de seigle. Il permit en son temps, de réduire les impôts sur le whiskey en contournant la taxe sur le malt. Aujourd'hui ce style de whiskey est produit au sein de la distillerie Midleton, située au sud de l'Irlande.

QUAICH : timbale à deux anses traditionnelle où l'on sert le whisky, notamment pour souhaiter la bienvenue à quelqu'un que l'on reçoit. Généralement en étain ou en inox, il peut se comparer en France au tastevin.

REFILL : en Écosse ou en Irlande, se dit d'un fût qui a déjà été utilisé au moins une fois pour faire vieillir le whisky (par opposition au first fill).

SINGLE MALT : whisky de malt provenant d'une seule et unique distillerie.

SINGLE CASK : mise en bouteilles d'un whisky issu d'un seul et unique fût.

VATTED/BLENDED MALT : single malts sélectionnés au sein de différentes distilleries de malts et mélangés entre eux.

SCOTCH WHISKY : whisky produit, élevé et embouteillé en Écosse, à partir de céréales, distillé dans des alambics et vieilli dans des fûts de chêne pour une période minimum de trois ans. Le degré minimum d'un scotch est de 40 % vol.

SHERRY BUTT : fût de chêne d'une capacité variant de 500 à 700 litres, utilisé pour l'élevage des vins de Jerez de la Frontera et les sherries. Il existe différentes variétés de vin de sherry : fino, manzanilla, amontillado, oloroso, pedro ximenez. Les ex-fûts de sherry les plus recherchés par les distilleries sont les olorosos et les pedros ximenez.

SMALL BATCH : assemblage de plusieurs whiskies provenant d'un petit nombre de fûts différents.

TOURBE : composant organique résultant de la décomposition partielle de végétaux. Une fois découpée en briquettes et séchée, la tourbe fournit un combustible qui va parfumer certains malts.

UN-CHILLFILTERED : « non filtré à froid ». Whiskies non filtrés à froid, afin de préserver le maximum d'acides gras, à l'origine d'une texture douce et soyeuse. Ces whiskies présentent généralement un degré égal ou supérieur à 46 % vol.

WHISKY : « eau-de-vie » de grain, d'un volume d'alcool minimum de 40 % vol., élevé en fût de chêne.

Printed in China by Toppan Leefung in July 2017
Achevé d'imprimer par Toppan Leefung (Chine) en juillet 2017